WESLEYAN THEO

# BE HOLY

*Compliments of*

Wesleyan Education Council

~

Education and the Ministry

~

Wesleyan Publishing House

Wesleyan Theological Perspectives

# BE HOLY

## *God's Invitation to Understand, Declare, and Experience Holiness*

Edited by Joseph Coleson

Indianapolis, Indiana

Published by Wesleyan Publishing House
Indianapolis, Indiana 46250
Printed in the United States of America
ISBN: 978-0-89827-372-4

To the memory of all God's saints who have led us into biblical holiness by example and by word, in pulpit, pew, and classroom, who now enjoy God's holiness in fullness both of understanding and of experience, this volume is dedicated with utmost respect and continuing affection.

# CONTENTS

# FOREWORD

The exhortation of 1 Peter 1:15–16, "But just as he who called you is holy, so be holy in all you do; for it is written: 'Be holy, because I am holy,'" is both a convicting and a compelling message that has not changed through the centuries. It still conveys the optimism of God's grace available to address the deepest needs of the human heart, along with—or, better, including—the cultural issues of our day. Holiness is the message of hope, just as relevant today as it was when Peter challenged the early church.

The mission of the Wesleyan Movement from the start has been to "proclaim the message of scriptural holiness." The phrase "Called unto Holiness" describes much more than a hymn we sing; it is a call woven throughout the tapestry of Scripture to denote who we are as the people of God. As Peter wrote, "But you are a chosen people, a royal priesthood, a holy nation, a people belonging to God, that you may declare the praises of him who called you out of darkness into his wonderful light" (1 Pet. 2:9).

Holiness is and always should be an identifiable trait of God's people. Holy people are called to be set apart for God's purposes in the world. The church must never drift away from or neglect to proclaim this message. Holiness still is our mission, holiness both personal and corporate.

This book illuminates and inspires renewed confidence in this wonderful message of holiness. The opening chapter compellingly urges the church to reclaim and rediscover the awesome truth that God's grace makes it possible for men and women to be holy people.

Holiness is the compelling message that God can transform the human heart and enable people to live holy lives.

Chapters 2 and 3 unfold both thoughtfully and inspirationally the Old and New Testament primary definition of holiness as relational. That is, holiness is separation *to* God as our first and most important relationship; the initiative is God's, but humanly, it is based in our response to God's invitation to family membership and intimacy, and in our willing, eager acceptance of God's *torah* (instruction). This leads naturally to human relationships of integrity, fidelity, and mutual lovingkindness (*hesed*). The approaches taken by these two authors are quite different. This is intentional, partly to illustrate that holiness is not a concept spun artificially out of a reluctant text, but rather, when correctly understood, is part and parcel, warp and woof, the beginning and the end, of the biblical report of God's intentions toward humankind.

With the scriptural basis clearly in focus, successive chapter authors present excellent treatments of the historical and theological understandings of holiness, beginning with the invaluable contributions of John and Charles Wesley. Then the developmental impact of Wesleyan-holiness theology and practice on the American scene is clarified, followed by an examination of holiness in other Christian traditions, notably the Roman Catholic and the Eastern Orthodox communions.

Upon this strong biblical, historical, and theological foundation, the remaining chapters address, with a rare combination of acuity and warmth, the practical implications of the holiness message in pastoral preaching and teaching, personal experience, spiritual disciplines, corporate and community life, and the impact of holiness as a catalyst for transformational change in society. The full range of what it means to be "holiness people" is included, from the personal, individual assent to and pursuit of holiness, to the centrality of holiness in the life of a healthy congregation, to a stirring call to rekindle the global vision and action that are the hallmarks of biblical holiness that once defined the

Wesleyan Holiness Movement and that we are beginning, once again, to hear and respond to. On this point that *all* of it is "holiness," we dare not surrender, as we did so disastrously about a hundred years ago. For this reason, you will see some of our holiness ancestors and important events in our history referenced several times; you will read some ideas propounded, expounded, and urged more than once, by several authors. Think of it as a chorus of united voices reminding us of the beauty of holiness when we see and proclaim it whole, not in fragments.

This book will become standard reading for ministers and laity alike, as we pick up again with rekindled energy our calling to own, articulate, and practice the message of holiness, personally and communally. It will propel the church to be true to its identity and mission purpose. The holiness message is central; it comprises the DNA of who we are as Wesleyans. This book will stamp a lasting imprint on individuals and churches—an inspiring and compelling reminder to be who we are, truly the people of God. I hope and pray it impacts your personal life to every nook and corner; I hope and pray it renews, revitalizes, and transforms your ministry.

THOMAS E. ARMIGER
General Superintendent
The Wesleyan Church

1

# THE JOURNEY

*David W. Holdren*

*For in Christ Jesus neither circumcision nor uncircumcision has any value. The only thing that counts is faith expressing itself through love.*

—Galatians 5:6

*We so preach faith in Christ as not to supercede, but produce holiness . . . [faith] is still only the handmaid of love.*

—John Wesley

Over the years, the list of beliefs I hold without reservation has grown shorter. I simply am not as sure as I used to be about some of the doctrines detailing our perceptions of how God works in us. Reducing the list has not been the result of becoming more of a doubter, nor has it been due to losing confidence in God, the Bible, or the Christian way; in these, my confidence soars.

My uncertainties have more to do with the doctrinal detailing of our transformational journey. My experiences simply don't match up to the clearly formulated pathway often described in certain expressions of Wesleyan theology. Typically, our holiness doctrines leave inadequate room for customization in God's work with the individual. The profound differences of capacity and experience that shape each of us affect how we process life, a fact I believe is not lost on God.

The Bible is not a book of systematic theology. It is a book that chronicles the work of the Father, Son, and Holy Spirit with individuals and groups of people. Genesis, for example, is basically God's activities with several generations of the family of Abraham. Our theologies, at times, may interfere with our discernment of God's intentions for us and his instructions to us. Doctrines are *derived* postulates of truth and are influenced by numerous aspects of the human condition.

Do I disdain doctrine? Absolutely not. Doctrinal formulations help correlate and integrate various portions of God's Word on a particular issue, which helps avoid "proof-texting" our views. Theology is the result of homework that few of us would do, benefits all of us through the expertise that only a few of us have, and gives us frameworks for truth that all of us need.

This need is apparent already from New Testament times. First John, for example, was written specifically to correct errors about Christ and Christianity that were gaining acceptance in the early days. John's clear and strong correctives indeed may have saved the day for the young Christian movement.

However, even with the merits of doctrine and doctrinal teaching clearly in mind, it is difficult for theologians to fashion them without being affected by their various traditions, reactions to doctrinal "competition," personal experience, interpretive decisions, and our fondest desires for human destiny.

Thus, it seems good to gather around our traditional expressions of core beliefs periodically and put them through the gauntlets of Scripture, reason, and experience. We need to ask, do the terms, phrases, and analogies we have used historically still serve us well? Has theology gone so far in organizing our views of such things as the "how" of God's work with humankind that we have restricted the flow of God's grace?

## WHY THE HOLINESS MOVEMENT DIED

Over a period of 120 years or so, a clear and growing movement of churches held holiness as their core tenet. For a time, the movement produced great energy by strong preaching and clear challenges to holy living. But now, even though many of those denominations and organizations still exist, the movement does not.

Let me suggest some reasons for its demise. Holiness preaching too often was overstated and too often under-lived. It focused on externals and extremes. It became believer-centered rather than Christ-centered. It had God so well figured out, in terms of what God did and how God did it on the journey to holiness, that it left God little room to work in God's uniquely personal ways with each individual.

Frankly, many of us who were earnest seekers in the Wesleyan tradition found we were not experiencing levels of deliverance, godliness, joy, and love in the precise formulations preached and expected. Some of the terms and phrases that had become sacred to holiness people have about the same effect for our generation, and for those following us, as trying to drive the family car down the freeway on four flat tires.

*Eradication* is one example; it refers to the destruction or cleansing of one's sinning nature. Certainly the Bible affirms cleansing from all sin, a cleansing that is real and available for us. It is not specific, however, about inclination and capacity for sin. Can God deliver us from a spirit of rebellion toward him? Absolutely. Does God systematically deliver us from the power of temptations leading to sin? Apparently not. Do Christians need to be dominated by the power of sin controlling our lives? Absolutely not. However, trust and obedience are the ingredients God joins to deliver us, rather than a one-time repair of human nature. What God said to Cain still applies to you and me: "Sin is crouching at your door; it desires to have you, but you must master it" (Gen. 4:7).

*Second work of grace* is another common phrase many Wesleyans still freely use and defend. This phrase is an assertion that there is a point in time when God sanctifies a person. Yet it could slight the amazing flow of God's grace always at work in our lives in a multitude of ways.

*Christian perfection* is another; it was and is intended to relate more to a pure heart and proper intention than to flawless performance. However, in our culture the term "perfection" primarily relates to flawlessness, thus providing an initial barrier or resistance to the intended meaning of the phrase. Besides, the watching public is quite aware of some of the flaws of those of us who preach holiness and perfection.

*Entire sanctification* probably is the dominant phrase representing the heart of holiness theology among Wesleyans. Many, both inside and outside holiness circles, have wondered, however, how anyone can be entirely *anything* when so much of life is yet to be lived. What is *entire* about entire sanctification?

## SO, THEN, WHY HOLINESS?

Despite our issues with some earlier holiness phraseology, we Wesleyans continue to affirm the importance of holiness as a biblical and Christian doctrinal understanding. Why?

First, holiness is significant and urgent for us because it is a major consideration of the Bible. One example, out of many references, is Hebrews 12:14: "Make every effort to live in peace with all men and to be holy; without holiness no one will see the Lord." That sounds as though we need to give holiness careful consideration!

A second reason for pursuing holiness is that it is good for us. Contrary to some popular opinions, to be a holy person is not nearly so much a subtraction as it is an addition to our lives. Holiness includes the idea of an integrated, whole, and healthy life. Pursuit of God's design for our holiness addresses issues of our identity, significance, and meaningful contribution in this life.

A third reason is "because." Peter exhorts us, "But just as he who called you is holy, so be holy in all you do; for it is written: 'Be holy, because I am holy'" (1 Pet. 1:15–16). Holiness is a call to be like our heavenly Father. It is a challenge to be restored in his image, and the best example of God's image is the Son, Jesus Christ. Therefore, holiness is Christlikeness.

A fourth reason picks up where the last one leaves off. The world *expects* holiness from us! The world longs to see Christlike lives and Christian character where the walk matches the talk. In the aftermath of the revelations of sexual abuse in the Roman Catholic Church, as well as other churches, what do we suppose the average citizen thinks about what is important for priests and preachers? Is it better sermons, rosaries, Communion, or confession booths? No! They want spiritual leaders and Christ-followers who live up to their calling! I contend that even the world celebrates those serving a holy God, who *live* like it. In the words of Paul's exhortation, we are to "live a life worthy of the calling" (Eph. 4:1).

Finally, holiness makes us what Christ says we are and need to be: salt and light in this world. Salt has a purifying and flavoring influence. Light has a revealing, colorful, and guiding effect. A holy life is suited to accomplish all that and more!

God calls each of us to be more than merely forgiven. God calls us to become like himself, as we see him in Christ (Eph. 5:1). It sounds like a "mission impossible," but it is not; God does not set us up for failure.

If you are a fairly new Christian—or if you are not—your mind may be swirling as you ponder the meaning of the salvation-sanctification terms mentioned in this book. As we approach the "how" issue, let us clarify some distinctions between the Christian terms *salvation* and *sanctification*.

## HOW ARE SALVATION AND SANCTIFICATION DIFFERENT?

Consider marriage as our analogy, since it is the one used in Ephesians 5. When I got married, my delight was primarily about what, or whom, I was *getting*. I claimed this wonderful woman, all for *myself*. She was *mine*. She met *my* criteria and would surely meet *my* needs and expectations. Do you see a theme here? It was mainly about the great deal *I was getting*.

Similarly, initial motives for becoming a Christian often center on the great deal *I am getting*, at God's expense. God provides the love and grace. Christ did the dying for my sins, and God extends mercy and forgiveness to all who believe on him. I receive eternal life. My past is no longer held against me. I receive Christ as my Savior. Do you see a theme here? Salvation, too, is mainly about the great deal *I am getting*.

If two people in a marriage plow ahead insisting that all their own expectations be met, their own needs fulfilled, that marriage likely is headed for trouble. Marriages that thrive are the ones in which both partners eventually realize the need to make a second kind of vow. In spite of the struggles and the imperfections each now clearly sees in the spouse, both make a deep-level consecration to the marriage and to loving that partner, regardless of effort, sacrifice, and cost. Though many marriages begin as a kind of relational salvation, their ultimate success depends on a kind of "sanctification." Marriages thrive on eliminating marriage "sins," and developing faithfulness in love and contribution.

In the same way, as we attempt to grow in Christ, we normally become quite aware that a lot of "me" keeps getting in the way of doing what Jesus would have us do. The Bible sometimes refers to the "me" factor as the "flesh," the flawed human nature, inclining me to sin and ungodly character. We need help (see Rom. 7:7–35).

Personal sanctification is needed for the Christian to thrive. In what may be an over-simplification, salvation depends on Christ as our *Savior*; sanctification seeks to establish Christ as the *Lord* of our life.

The terms *sanctify* and *holy* both come from the same Hebrew root in the Old Testament, and from the same Greek word in the New Testament; both mean "to be separate, set apart, dedicated" for God's use. The early essence of being sanctified relates to one's attitude and orientation to God through Christ.

By extension, these words also carry the meaning of being purified, or cleansed, for sacred use. Paul challenged Timothy to flee evil and pursue righteousness (1 Tim. 6:11). In Ephesians, his admonition is "to put off your old self, which is being corrupted by its deceitful desires . . . and to put on the new self, created to be like God in true righteousness and holiness" (4:22–24).

In many other terms, phrases, and analogies, the Bible describes sanctification as a combination of deliverance and dedication, all of which happens in partnership with God. John Wesley loved Paul's expression of the heart of holiness in the words "The only thing that counts is faith expressing itself through love" (Gal. 5:6).

Wesley also considered love the essential fruit or outworking of holiness, so he had strong regard for the words of Jesus as a key description of the goals of holy living: "'Love the Lord your God with all your heart and with all your soul and with all your mind.' This is the first and greatest commandment. And the second is like it: 'Love your neighbor as yourself'" (Matt. 22:37–39).

## HOW DO WE PROGRESS FROM SALVATION TO SANCTIFICATION?

Holiness is about being imitators of God—more specifically, about being Christlike. Most branches of the Christian faith have teachings on holiness, but they vary widely in their understanding of the degree to which a person can experience the sanctified life here and now, and how it is attained.

One theory says it all happens when a person first comes to Christ in faith. This writer believes (with most Wesleyans) that, yes, all things are possible with God, but human nature and need suggest that inviting Christ into our lives as Savior and surrendering to Christ as Lord are two very different issues. Even so, Wesleyan views of sanctification are optimistic, to varying degrees. Let's return to the marriage analogy.

At what point in a marriage is each partner *entirely* married? It is a fair question, for the sake of marriage, and for a discussion of sanctification. Both marriage and sanctification share the notion of a person being "set apart" for specific and holy purpose. It involves a kind of total dedication.

So, when *are* two people entirely married? Is it at the official pronouncement of the marriage by agents of the church or state? Does the state of being entirely married occur at some mystical moment during the marriage, but subsequent to the wedding? Or can two people ever be entirely married until their final moments of life on earth?

As for sanctification, holiness denominations generally have held one of three basic positions concerning its entirety and when it occurs.

The *shorter way* is the most optimistic view. This view says a Christian can experience entire sanctification now, in the present moment. It comes as one surrenders the total self to God. God then purifies the surrendered one from sin and its nature within, enabling one to love and obey him with all one's being. This view sees sanctification primarily as an event in which God does most of what happens, and which is completed in a moment of time.

The *middle way* is a view suggesting the Christian is not able simply to exercise faith at will for God to sanctify the heart and life.

One needs to have a fairly clear grasp of one's need and a growing passion to pursue holiness. This view sees entire sanctification as a combination of clear acts of consecration and response, coupled with discipline, repentance, growth, and maturity over time. Sanctification is a partnership in which both God *and* the individual have clear and distinct responsibilities. Sanctification is sustained and built upon over the course of a life lived faithfully and in utter responsiveness to the leadings of God's Word and Spirit.

An important point is that the "shorter way" distinguishes between Christian maturity and Christian holiness. It holds that a person could be entirely sanctified, yet not be spiritually mature. By contrast, the "middle way" sees a stronger connection between maturity and holiness.

Third is the *longer way*. It views entire sanctification as occurring only after a long journey of dying to oneself, of discipline, of growing in grace, and of maturing to the point of truly understanding the meaning of entire sanctification. In this view, Christian maturity is what really makes one ready for entire sanctification. It is more a process than an instantaneous event, and setbacks are not uncommon. There may be a greater emphasis on suppression of sin than on once-for-all-time deliverance from sin. In this less optimistic view, entire sanctification may be seen as most likely to occur shortly before or at the moment of death.[1]

Although John and Charles Wesley both longed for holiness in this life, they disagreed on when and how much of it one could expect here on earth. John was an intelligent and intense man, disciplined and driven. Around 1760, he began to wonder whether his expectations for the level of deliverance from sin that he taught others were too severe, becoming more a bondage than a freedom. In his earlier years, John had preached an entirety in sanctification that was immediate and complete (the "shorter way"), but in these later years, he stressed more process and growth in holiness (the "middle way"). Charles retained a lofty expectation for one's level of sanctification, but believed it could be attained only at death (the "longer way").

## DISCONTENT, DEDICATION, DELIVERANCE, DISCIPLINE

Let me propose now that sanctification leading to a holy life flows from four aspects of experience: *discontent*, *dedication*, *deliverance*, and *discipline*. Furthermore, all this is the interaction of a divine-human partnership. Some aspects of sanctification only God can accomplish in us. Some things he will not do for us. Let us, then, worry less about what God does, and focus more on what the Bible and the Holy Spirit say we need to do in the divine-human partnership.

*Discontent.* As noted earlier, a person comes to Christ out of a sense of need. We need forgiveness from sins committed, we want Christ in our lives, and we want eternal life. All these are valid prompters to come to Christ in faith. We are born again to a new life, focused in a new direction.

However, three enemies are opposed to our new life: the world, the flesh, and the devil. By these we mean, respectively, the ungodly forms of influence that manifest themselves daily in our world; the aspects of our human nature that are bent toward pride and self-centeredness; and Satan, the ultimate personal force of evil in the universe.

Besides this "unholy trinity," we also contend with a multitude of pressures from our past and with those of daily life. We struggle with impure motives and thoughts. Our words and actions sometimes sink below basic expectations for a Christian. It can seem that the harder we try, the deeper into defeat we go. The Christian life is not working out as we had hoped. Ironically, this discontent can give rise to a new day!

At this point, repentance is our ally. Repentance is about taking a good look at the way things have been and declaring our discontent. We long for life on a higher plane, doing what Jesus would have us do.

*Dedication.* North American Christians often talk about "accepting Christ," or "trusting in Jesus," or "receiving Christ." It almost sounds as though we were doing God a favor, though we do not intend it that way. Rarely is the notion of self-sacrifice or personal surrender to God considered in these early stages of Christianity. We prefer the benefits without much cost. We too often are bent on "cheap grace," that is, on forgiveness without repentance, on Christianity without Christlikeness, on deliverance without discipline.

At some point, we need to make a clear and conscious shift from a self-oriented life to a Christ-oriented one. Paul put it this way: "I urge you . . . in view of God's mercy, to offer your [selves] as living sacrifices, holy and pleasing to God—this is your spiritual act of worship. Do not conform any longer to the pattern of this world, but be transformed by the renewing of your mind" (Rom. 12:1–2). This is a call for total dedication and transformation, accomplished as God and we do our parts.

It is virtually impossible for a marriage to survive when two individuals are determined that the relationship exists to meet their own needs. Only when both persons in the marriage truly consecrate, or dedicate, themselves to the other person and to the relationship can the marriage thrive.

We first trust in Christ as our Savior. Eventually, we learn God calls us to crown Christ as Lord of our lives. We declare a lifelong yes to what God wants and follow hard after the character of Christ, as his Spirit helps us (Gal. 5:22–23; 1 Cor. 13:4–8).

*Discipline.* Discussions about sanctification and holiness often focus on what God does for us to make us holy. An outstanding example of this is 1 John 1:9: "If we confess our sins, he is faithful and just and will forgive us our sins and purify us from all unrighteousness." Another is Paul's prayer in 1 Thessalonians 5:23: "May God himself, the God of peace, sanctify you through and through. May your whole spirit, soul and body be kept blameless at the coming of our Lord Jesus Christ." These things we believe God does.

However, there is a long-underrated secret to a holy life: *self-discipline for God's sake*. I cannot express it more strongly than by quoting only a few of many scriptural exhortations: "For God did not give us a spirit of timidity, but a spirit of power, of love and of *self-discipline*" (2 Tim. 1:7, emphasis added); "Let us *purify ourselves* from everything that contaminates body and spirit, perfecting holiness out of reverence for God" (2 Cor. 7:1, emphasis added); "You were taught . . . to put off your old self, which is being corrupted by its deceitful desires; to be made new in the attitude of your minds; and to put on the new self, created to be like God in true righteousness and holiness" (Eph. 4:22–24).

Remember, the Christian life, the holy life, is a loving and disciplined partnership between God and us. One final aspect of sanctification makes it all possible.

*Deliverance.* If the sanctified life reflects Christ, then whose help do we need to achieve it? We need the Spirit of Christ at work in us. As Paul said, "Now the Lord is the Spirit, and where the Spirit of the Lord is, there is freedom" (2 Cor. 3:17).

All the self-management, self-control, and self-discipline in the world will not lead us to the level of living that can be achieved when we are daily surrendered to and focused on God's Holy Spirit helping our human spirit. The Spirit guides us, prods us, and even cooperates to transform us from the inside out. The outcomes of God's work inside us are partially described in Galatians 5:22–23. Take a look at that wonderful list of character and behavior traits.

Jesus gave numerous illustrations from nature to describe spiritual dynamics. Although this is not one of his, we may compare the cleansing from sin issue to the ways different trees get rid of dead leaves. Dead leaves are analogous to those thoughts, habits, attitudes, behaviors, or tendencies that no longer belong in our Christian life.

Some trees, like the sugar maple, shed their leaves at the first wave of frost. One day the tree is full of color, the next, it is almost bare. Other trees hold their leaves a bit longer until the rain and wind drive them off. Some aspects of our old nature are like that. Certain things just fall away when we come to Christ. Other tendencies and ungodly characteristics take some time and effort to dispatch.

Then there is the pin oak. Its leaves, though dead and dry, continue to cling through the winter winds, through the rain and snow, until spring. When new life surges into the tree, the old leaves drop off. When we invite God's Spirit to infect our own, an expulsive power is born. As with trees, so with us; total cleansing is not a single or simple process, because of the nature of life and our needs. Some things are resolved quickly, without much battle; others require effort; still others can be driven off only by the "expulsive" impact of our willingness and the Spirit's power.

## ENTIRELY SANCTIFIED AND IN PROCESS

A holy life is one of consecration, cleansing, increasingly Christlike character, and contribution. It is intended to affect every relationship in our lives, for all the days of our lives.

Now, to return to our earlier question and to complete our analogy, when are two people *entirely* married? Is it at the completion of the wedding ceremony? In one sense, the answer is yes. Yet, though completed in the legal sense, the marriage is far from complete with regard to its growth and maturity. Apart from attainment of the maturity and saving graces of any good relationship, the marriage will lack fulfillment; it even may lack faithfulness. In yet another sense, the marriage is not entire or complete until the final day of that couple, the day of the death of one of them. Then and only then is it complete.

Just so, God's work (grace) is never finished or completed in our lives until we leave this earth. Our holiness is never entire or complete, in one sense, until our final breath is exhaled.

Yet, there is a sense in which we can experience "entire sanctification." It is found in presenting *all* of myself to God (Rom. 12:1), for *all* the days of my life, and learning to love God with *all* my heart, soul, and strength, and to love my neighbor as myself. It is, at that point, entire and complete in intention and declaration. Then we validate that in practice as we daily walk in responsiveness to Christ and to the Word of God.

As we grow in faith and love, we also grow in the hope of God's willingness and power to make possible what at first seemed impossible!

The call is clear. The journey is worth it. The results are good for everyone! Are you willing? Are you ready?

## ACTION/REFLECTION SUGGESTIONS

**1.** Reflect on your most important relationships. Determine in each relationship whether you are primarily a "giver" or a "taker." If you are married, what about your marriage? What about you and God? In what sense is "satisfaction" needed on your part?

**2.** In what ways do you tend to "lose it" as a Christian—regarding your behavior, attitudes, emotions, and words? Using the dead-leaves analogy, what might help you keep it together better?

**3.** Regarding a holy life, how do the terms *discontent*, *dedication*, *deliverance*, and *discipline* relate to your needs and experience? How would you like your Christian life to be different, in a positive way? What do you suppose it would take for that to happen?

## NOTE

1. I am indebted to Professor Chris Bounds of Indiana Wesleyan University for my understanding of the "shorter," "middle," and "longer" ways, though the concepts are older.

# OLD TESTAMENT FOUNDATIONS

*Joseph Coleson*

*For I am* Yahweh *your God; now sanctify yourselves,*
*and* be *holy, for I am holy.*

—Leviticus 11:44[1]

*Had he [man] not been a free as well as an intelligent being,*
*his understanding would have been as incapable of holiness,*
*or any kind of virtue, as a tree or a block of marble.*

—John Wesley

On his morning break, Shawn called his pastor and asked whether he could see him later that afternoon. Pastor Jones said four o'clock would work for him.

Shawn got right to the point. "Pastor, I've been seeing four different women regularly over the last ten months. I love them all, for different reasons. Why can't I just marry them all?"

Some cultures have tried that approach to marriage; some continue to practice it, but always with disappointing-to-disastrous results. Yet, when it comes to matters of faith, some moderns and postmoderns think that just such a picking and choosing of the best from a smorgasbord of religions and traditions of spirituality is an apt approach to building a personal faith.

A common reason this approach to religious faith may seem rational is that we almost always approach faith from the wrong end. This is true of most of popular Christianity, as well as of other religious and spiritual traditions. When we think "religion," or "faith," we think first "morality" or "ethics." And from that entry point, most traditions and systems can look pretty much alike.

But a biblical faith is not *first* about moral and ethical probity. Biblical faith is about faith in *God*. This is not just any god, either; it is the personal God *Yahweh* of the Old Testament, as disclosed fully in Jesus Christ, who is prophesied in the Old Testament and revealed in the New. Biblical faith is first and foremost about the intimate relationship this God passionately desires with every human.

The long and the short of it is this: Biblical holiness is about separation—but separation as a positive concept, not a negative one. With respect to God, holiness means God is separate from God's creation, not part of it. The theological word for this is *transcendence*. With respect to God's people, biblical, Christian holiness means we are separate *to* God, and the preposition is important!

Because this concept is central, and because we so often distort it, slide over it, or simply miss it, we will take time to demonstrate that we no more can divide our spiritual loyalties, with integrity, than Shawn can marry all four of the women he says he "loves."

## THE HEBREW WORD *QADASH*

It is not too much to say that when we understand this idea correctly and fully, the epigraphs at the head of this chapter represent *the* dual theme of Christian Scripture from Genesis 1 to Revelation 22: God is holy; God invites God's people to be holy.

*Qadash: Separated, Consecrated, Sanctified, Holy.* If this is so—and this chapter is a partial attempt to demonstrate that it is—we need to know what "holy" means. Because it is the root most directly and correctly translated "holy," and because it occurs about 850 times in the Old Testament (almost once per chapter), we will begin with the Hebrew word *qadash*. (If you have no Hebrew, please bear with me; this will not be nearly as complex as it may seem at first glance.)

First, we must get in our heads firmly, without reservation, that the original and primary meaning of *qadash* is "consecration, surrender, or dedication"—that is, separation *to* "a deity."

The list of things that could be separated to a deity is nearly endless. Mountains, cities, temples, temple personnel and other human beings, altars of sacrifice, other temple furnishings and utensils, sacrificial offerings, gifts of money—all these and more are described as "holy" in the Bible and in other texts. All these entities share the common characteristic of being or having been consecrated, surrendered, to the deity and the deity's use. Except for human beings, none has the capacity for moral or ethical qualities.

*Deity Itself Is Holy.* But what about when the "thing" separated is the deity's own self? In Ugaritic texts, especially, but also in other inscriptions in other languages, Ba'al and other gods are called "holy." These texts definitely intended to locate the gods outside the common world of everyday human existence and usage.

The gods were larger than human—in their power, but more importantly, in their immortality. Their supposed freedom from permanent death was the attribute that finally set the gods apart from mere mortals and gave them unassailable power over us. If they *cannot* die and we *must* die, we must bow to their will, capricious or not. The holiness of the gods, their separateness from mortal humanity, consisted precisely and only in their immortality.[2]

## ISAIAH 6:3: A *CRUX INTERPRETUM*

On the surface, it would seem the Old Testament says the same thing about Israel's God. The most dramatic assertion of God's holiness in the Old Testament is the antiphonal refrain of the seraphim recorded in Isaiah 6:3: "*Qadosh, qadosh, qadosh*"—Holy, holy, holy—is *Yahweh* of hosts."[3] Certainly, the scene of Isaiah's Temple vision, the words spoken there, the event of Isaiah's call there, and the words chosen with great care to record all this converge to place the highest possible emphasis on God as the Holy One, without equal anywhere.

In Isaiah 6:3, however, we see something more than the theology of Israel's pagan neighbors merely applied to Israel's God, *Yahweh*. The whole verse reads, "*Qadosh, qadosh, qadosh* [Holy, holy, holy] is *Yahweh* of hosts. The fullness of all the earth is his glory."[4] The second statement is possible because of the first; it also partly defines the first. The second statement can be understood two ways; I believe Isaiah intended both.

The first meaning is that the fullness of all the earth *constitutes* the earthly manifestation of his glory. That is, the earth and all its systems show forth the glory of God, their Creator—the earth and we who are part of the earth are the glory of God insofar as we can experience it. Included here is not only the physical universe, but also all that humans can know and experience of God as we enter and grow in the grace of the redemption offered through Jesus Christ.

The second meaning is that the fullness of all the earth *consists* in his glory. That is, the earth and all its systems experience fullness—the fulfillment of all God created them to be, do, and relate to—only as, and insofar as, the glory of God fills and fulfills them. Put another way, that glory in, by, and through which *alone* the earth may be regarded as "full" or "fulfilled" is defined as "the glory of God." If the earth, or some part of it (including human beings) is not filled with and does not manifest the glory of God, it does not exist in the fullness—does not exhibit the glory—God intended for it.

No one would have said any of this of any of the pagan deities of Israel's neighbors. Isaiah 6:3 and many other statements and whole passages in Isaiah, Ezekiel, several of the psalms, and other places in the Hebrew Scripture are statements of or developments from the idea of the transcendence of Yahweh, Israel's God. As John Oswalt has shown, the concept of transcendence is not present in the theology of any of Israel's neighbors. Neither could Israel have "discovered" or "invented" transcendence unaided.[5] Transcendence is a revealed concept, the first concept necessary to understand God *as* God, and perhaps the most difficult concept for ancient Israel (or any people) to grasp and accept.

The idea of the holiness of God, therefore, is the idea of God's transcendence. The statement "God is holy" means, before anything else, "God is separate." How is God separate? God is separate by reason of being the transcendent One, that is, the preexistent One, the noncontingent One, the nondependent One, the unmade Maker, the One over and outside all creation, the Maker, Sustainer, and End of all.

Even the self-disclosed Divine Name attests this truth. Grammatically, the name *Yahweh* is from a "weak" Hebrew root. Because of this, the four Hebrew letters of the Divine Name—*yod*, *he*, *vav*, *he*—may be read as meaning either "he is/will be" or "he causes/will cause to be." As with the translation of Isaiah 6:3, above, I think this dual possibility is deliberate and should cause us always to think both/and. Yahweh is the transcendent One, the One who was/is/will be, *and* who caused/causes/will cause [all else] to be.

## GENESIS 1: A PROSE HYMN TO *'ELOHIM*

What really set my feet on the path to this understanding of God's holiness as transcendence was my early introduction to the authentic intent of Genesis 1. That this understanding of who God is should be so important as to stand at the head of the Jewish-Christian canon marks it as a *sine qua non*: without understanding and affirming the nature and character of God as presented in this very first entry in the Sacred Text, one cannot be truly Jewish or truly Christian.

What, then, is this crucial understanding from Genesis 1? It is precisely what we have been discussing: that God is, first and foremost, the transcendent One. That is the first truth Genesis 1 is set up to teach, the reason it contains what it contains and omits what it omits.

From the beginning to the end of their national existence, Israel was surrounded by pagan neighbors, each of whom worshiped various entities and forces of nature among their many gods. The best known and most powerful of these are presented in the Genesis 1 creation account, not as "gods," but as God's, not as deities at all, but as created servants of the transcendent One who brought them all into being and sustains them.

The first evidence is the claim of Genesis 1:1: "In the beginning God created the heavens and the earth." In the pagan theogonies of Israel's neighbors, every god was an entity in, or a force or process of, nature. By definition, none could be transcendent, nor could any have brought into being all else that is. Yet that is precisely the claim of Genesis 1:1 for *'Elohim*, identified in Genesis 2 as *Yahweh 'Elohim*, Yahweh who is God, the transcendent One.

In the best-known and most detailed extrabiblical creation account, the Akkadian *Enuma Elish*, Ti'amat was the goddess personifying the chaotic storm-nature of the waters of the primeval deep. In that account, the young god Marduk engaged Ti'amat in single combat, defeated and killed her, and created the earth and its atmosphere from the two halves of her body, which he had split "like a shellfish." Yet, Genesis 1:2 affirms, "Now as for the earth, it was [at first] nonproductive and empty, and darkness was upon the face of the *tehom* [the deep], and [or: but] the *ruach 'Elohim* [wind/breath/Spirit of God] was brooding upon the face of the waters." In the Mesopotamian account, the waters of the primeval deep (Ti'amat) threatened to destroy even the gods. In the Genesis account, the waters of the primeval deep (*tehom*—the same Semitic root as Ti'amat) were not a goddess; they were not even chaotic or stormy. As God's wind/breath/Spirit hovered over them, they waited quietly for God's first creative act upon the surface of the earth. God (*Elohim*) is the transcendent One.

Among most of Israel's neighbors, the sea (*yam*) was a powerful god, amenable to no one's direction. In Genesis 1:9–10, God merely spoke to the waters, commanding them to gather themselves into one place, and they complied. God is the transcendent One.

In the Akkadian *Enuma Elish*, humans were created from the blood of a guilty and executed rebel god, mixed with mud, to serve the victorious gods and thus alleviate the drudgery of the defeated and enslaved gods who had taken Ti'amat's side in the rebellion against Marduk. In Genesis 1 and 2, the human race, *'adam*, was created "in the image" and "likeness" of God, created male and female in a federal caretaking stewardship over the earth, created for fellowship with God and with each other. God, the transcendent One, here is revealed also as God the immanent One, coming "down" daily for intimate communion with the beloved first parents (Gen. 3:8).

Whatever the authorial and redactional history of the Genesis creation account, it reached its present final form, and its full final canonical status, during the Judean exile in Babylon, where Marduk reigned as supreme deity of the powerful pagan city and its empire. For such a time as this, God brought the real theology of creation to the forefront of Jewish spiritual consciousness, impressing upon them the vital truth that God is holy, transcendent, not a part of the created order, but Creator and Sustainer of all.

## YOU SHALL BE HOLY

Not only do the Hebrew Scriptures teach that God is holy. They record many times God's instruction that God's people are to be holy as well.

*Called to Be Holy.* The clearest, most direct instruction occurs in passages such as Leviticus 19:2: "Holy shall you be, for holy am I, *Yahweh* your God." "Holy" is the first word of both Hebrew clauses. This is one important way biblical Hebrew marks emphasis, by putting at the beginning a word that normal syntax would place farther down in the clause. This is not some do-it-if-it's-convenient sort of suggestion. Holiness is God's primary instruction for God's people: first, because of the syntactical emphasis just noted; second, by the parallelism prescribed in the instruction. God's people are to be holy *because* God is holy. God is holy; *therefore*, God's people are to be holy.

Of course, this instruction is not limited to Leviticus 19:2. Leviticus 18—26 is called the "Holiness Code" because it refers so often to God as holy, and so often instructed Israel they too were to be holy, because God is holy. Explicitly or implicitly, this instruction runs, not only throughout the Holiness Code of Leviticus, but through the rest of the Old Testament and the New as well.

*Created to Be Holy.* The rules of biblical interpretation do not allow us suddenly to veer off here onto another track. If *qadash* means "separate" when referring to God, it also must mean "separate" when referring to any other created entities that are or may become holy. Now, obviously, only God is transcendent, and transcendence is the characteristic by which we have defined God's essential holiness. Since we are not and cannot be *that*, how can humans ever be holy?

The answer is simple: We still can be "separate." In fact, all humans ultimately *must be* separate (read "holy") to someone or something. It is our destiny; we always are moving toward that to which or to whom we ultimately are becoming holy (read "separate"). We can do no other.

Remember Shawn? He's going to have to become "holy" (separate) to one of the four women he's dating, and let the others go.

Furthermore, he needs to do this fairly soon, or they will make the choice for him, and he may not get the chance to become separate to any one of them.

With respect to marriage, it is possible to be truly separate only to one spouse. Many individuals are "holy" to one leisure activity. When he's not working, you'll find him on the lake or river, fishing; you'll find her on the golf course; you'll find them in the garden. The deeper one's "holiness" to something or someone, the more likely other interests will be crowded out.

The point is not that any of these things is wrong or evil in itself. They are, in fact, the good gifts of God! Evil occurs when we worship and therefore misuse them, when we have "traded the truth of God for the lie, and reverenced and served the creature in place of the Creator" (Rom. 1:25). We are designed to worship God, and God alone.

However, worship as immobilized awe in abject subjection is not God's goal. God's zealous passion for the human race is that we will reciprocate God's love and enjoy the unending bliss of intimate relationship with God, here and hereafter. Appropriately intimate relationships with other humans, and with the rest of God's creation, also are included in God's intentions.

*Finding the Better Analogies.* Thus, the best analogy for God's ultimate intention certainly is not that of Sovereign and subject, though Wesleyans affirm as stoutly as any others that God is sovereign, noncontingent, and nondependent; while we are subject, contingent, and continuously dependent. But if that were all God wanted, any race of nonrational creatures or of slaves would suffice.

The better analogies are the ultimate biblical family analogies: God is Father (and Mother); Jesus Christ, second person of the Godhead, is the Elder Brother who has redeemed us or, even more intimately, the Bridegroom who has made us his heavenly bride; God the Holy Spirit "bears witness with our spirit that we are children of

God; and if children, then heirs, heirs of God and heirs with Christ" (Rom. 8:16–17). Here, the familiar proverbs of family resemblance—"like father, like son"; "like mother, like daughter"—can help us understand holiness as our (growing) resemblance to the family into which we have been adopted (Rom. 8:15).

If we feel the need to, we *may* begin with the analogy of sovereign and citizen, because God is sovereign, and we are God's dependent creatures. But we should not therefore think of ourselves as lowly citizens in some far-off corner of the empire who never will see the King. No, by God's infinite grace we belong not in the cottage but in the palace. We may sleep in the hayloft sometimes, out of temporary necessity, or even as a lark, but we have our own bedroom in the mansion. We cannot imagine walking out, because we know that only here is life and love and joy forever. *This* is holiness as God made us to be holy, as God passionately desires us to be holy—separation *to* God as beloved sons and daughters!

## HOW THEN SHALL WE LEARN?

But what does this mean in the here-and-now? For one thing, it means not just getting, but being, a good relationship partner. Relationships of integrity (holiness) start with separation, consecration, devotion, and exclusivity of affection, but they don't end there.

This is where moral and ethical instruction and practice come in. We live in a fallen world. We have been redeemed from our state as fallen and rebellious creatures. We need to be taught how to live as holy sons and daughters.

*Lessons from Natural Revelation.* Some lessons are obvious. As we noted above, all cultures and religious systems teach the basic tenets of what some call the moral law: do not murder; do not commit adultery; do not steal; do not lie; practice virtue; do as you would be done by. With respect to others, practice the Golden Rule. With respect to self, practice the Golden Mean. Anyone practicing these consistently will be esteemed as highly virtuous.

But this world was (and is), and we are, so far gone we need to be taught the subtleties, taught how the principles apply when it comes down to cases. And in any case we have, to this point, completely left God out of the picture. If we stop with the obvious, morality and ethics are just as likely to have us bypassing the holy all over again, as they are to lead us to it.

*Torah: God's instruction in holiness.* The Hebrew word *torah* means "instruction." Capitalized as "Torah," it has come to designate the first five books of the Old Testament, what most Christians call the Pentateuch. In the Bible itself, however, the broader and basic meaning of "instruction" is used consistently, referring not only to the Pentateuch, but to all the Hebrew Scripture. In the New Testament period and beyond, Christians came to see and study the New Testament also as *torah*, God's instruction for God's people.

At this point, most modern Christians must unlearn a false dichotomy. The Bible itself recognizes no such distinction as the "ceremonial" versus the "moral" law. In case we miss it in the Old Testament itself, Jesus is our Teacher here. When asked to identify the greatest commandment, Jesus cited the *Shema*,[6] no doubt as expected. But Jesus continued without a break and quoted Leviticus 19:18: "The second is *like it*. 'You shall love your neighbor as yourself'" (Matt. 22:39, emphasis added). God's instruction to God's people does *not* teach one kind of ceremonial holiness toward God, the Old Testament forms of which have passed away, and another kind of moral, ethical holiness toward people, the Old Testament forms of which remain valid today. *That* kind of separation is not biblical holiness.

The key to understanding the so-called ceremonial law[7] is to see that it was intended to teach Israel (and us) that the holy God deserves holy worship. In an astounding display of grace, God chooses to dwell with God's people. The place of God's dwelling is a holy place, a sanctuary. One does not come sick or dirty or carelessly into God's presence in the sanctuary. One does not bring tainted or blemished offerings to God in the sanctuary. To be holy to God means we are committed to being, doing, and giving only our best to God.

## REFLECTING GODS, OR REFLECTING GOD

Morality and ethics as functions of holiness come into the picture because of the nature and character of the God to whom we are holy. We become like that to which we give ourselves.

Negative examples may make this more vivid at first, because we are not so experienced with them. The person whose life is "holy" to wealth becomes unable to make a decision, large or small, without measuring its potential to enrich or to ruin. The person whose life is "holy" to sexual expression becomes unable to relate to others as persons; they become objects for the potential gratification of one's sexual appetites.

Turning to the positive, when we read it fairly with respect to its original contexts of time and place, the Bible presents a clear picture of God as loving, merciful, just, moral, and ethical. The word portrait first presented in Exodus 34:6 is repeated numerous times, in whole or in part: "*Yahweh* is the God of mercy/compassion and grace, slow to anger, and abundant of [in] lovingkindness and faithfulness."

*This* is the God to whom we should run, not walk, in adoration and eagerness. *This* is the God whose "fear" is not abject terror, but reverential awe. *This* is the God we may trust, for "faithful lovingkindness" is God's central characteristic, God's natural, constant disposition toward us. After all, we are God's beloved children, first by creation, then, when *we* had turned away, by God's passionate purpose to redeem us fully and eternally. *This* is the God whose character we are called to emulate, to assume, and to reflect. Because the holy (transcendent) God is a (holy) moral God, God's holy people are called to be a moral people.

## ACTION/REFLECTION SUGGESTIONS

**1.** Read and study Genesis 1 and Isaiah 6 in light of God's holiness as discussed in this chapter. Journal your own thoughts as you study. Pray through these chapters, journaling your prayers and the thoughts they prompt.

**2.** Ask yourself what one action or attitude adjustment such a deeper, fuller understanding of God's transcendence and holiness may require in your life. What step(s) might you need to take to bring it about?

**3.** If you regularly have the privilege of preaching, research and count the times you have preached the holiness of God and the holiness of God's people from the Old Testament. Ask yourself: When am I going to start? How will I help the people God has entrusted to my pastoral care to know God as holy? How will I help them to desire and move toward a holy relationship with God and with God's people, above all else?

## NOTES

1. All biblical quotations in this chapter are the author's translation.

2. In the end, this is the major theological point of the important classic *The Epic of Gilgamesh*, an early Sumerian tale best known in its Akkadian versions and editions. The gods never were credited with omniscience, as *Gilgamesh* itself demonstrates.

3. Throughout the Old Testament, God's name is *Yahweh*; it occurs about 6,600 times.

4. The more traditional translation, "Holy, holy, holy is *Yahweh* of hosts; the whole earth is filled with his glory," is not wrong and would not negate our point here. Think of these translations also in terms of both/and, rather than either/or.

5. John N. Oswalt, "Golden Calves and the 'Bull of Jacob': The Impact on Israel of Its Religious Environment" in Avraham Gileadi ed., *Israel's Apostasy and Restoration: Essays in Honor of Roland K. Harrison* (Grand Rapids, Mich.: Baker, 1988), 9–18.

6. Deuteronomy 6:5: "You shall love *Yahweh* your God. . . ."

7. In technical usage in biblical and ancient Near Eastern studies, *cultic* means "religious," "liturgical," "having to do with worship." Obviously, then, all the many regulations about the Tabernacle (later, the Jerusalem Temple), the priesthood, the sacrifices, ritual cleanness and uncleanness, and so forth, are "cultic" laws or regulations.

3

# HOLINESS IN THE NEW TESTAMENT

*Terence Paige*

*You were washed, you were sanctified, you were justified in the name of the Lord Jesus Christ and by the Spirit of our God.*

—1 Corinthians 6:11

What, then is that holiness which is the true "wedding garment," the only qualification for glory? . . . It first, through the energy of God, worketh love to God and all mankind; and, by this love, every holy and heavenly temper.

—John Wesley

Terms for "holy" or "holiness"—adjectives, nouns, and verbs—occur some 275 times in the New Testament. What do these terms mean? Why was this concept so important for early Christians? And how can we translate these ideas into terms meaningful for modern Christians to help them live according to God's will?

Let's start with general definitions. The New Testament writers took over ideas of holiness from the Old Testament and from Judaism. In the Old Testament, two basic spheres of meaning make up the idea of "holy" when it is applied to created things. The oldest of these notions is that of "separate to, belonging to a deity," "devoted" to some divine purpose, not common or ordinary. The second notion is that of moral purity or righteousness.

The first meaning is illustrated by the fact that the Sabbath day is called "holy" (Ex. 20:8, 11)—meaning it is a day devoted especially to worship and thanks to God, and to rest. Obviously a "day" cannot make moral decisions, but it still can be "holy." This is the reason the people of Israel are referred to in the Old Testament as God's "holy ones" or "saints"—they are set apart or devoted to God, and belong to him. By the way, wherever "saint" occurs in the English Bible, it translates a Hebrew or Greek word that literally means "holy person." Our English word *saint* originates from the Latin *sanctus*, which also means "holy person." Israel, when gathered to worship God, is called "the assembly of the holy ones" (Ps. 89:5).

It is because Israel is *God's* people, meant to be in relationship with God and reflect the character of the awesome and righteous Creator, that the second meaning associated with holiness develops, namely, being righteous. But as Coleson argues (chapter 2), we cannot get these backward: A person does not get to belong to God by acting morally. The belonging comes first, as God's gift, and the lifestyle is to flow from that relationship (Lev. 19:1–2; Ex. 19:6).

A third category of meaning for the word *holy* is when it applies to God, when it indicates something of God's transcendence, his "other-ness." It points to God's awe-inspiring presence, powerful and dangerous to those who act inappropriately. Hence Isaiah, in his call narrative, described a vision of heavenly beings proclaiming God as "holy" (Isa. 6:1–3). This holy presence of God evoked a knowledge of uncleanness in Isaiah (the opposite of holiness) and a sense of fear at God's overwhelming presence.

We find these same three basic meanings in the way words for holiness are used in the New Testament also. First, a quick language lesson. In Greek many of the words relating to holiness come from a common stem. It is like the way the English word *telephone* can be used as a noun (the thing on your desk) or a verb (to telephone a friend). Thus, in Greek the words for "holy" or a "saint" (*hagios*), "holiness" (*hagiosunē*), "sanctification" or "consecration" (*hagiasmos*), and "sanctify," "make holy" (*hagiazō*) all are related. It is important to keep this in mind when looking at texts with related ideas, though in English the terms may be different.

## JESUS AND THE GOSPELS

The Gospels seldom use the typical holiness terms for people, with the notable exception of John 17 (see below). John the Baptist is described as a "holy man" in the opinion even of Herod Antipas (Mark 6:20), and the Old Testament prophets are described as "holy" in the song of Zechariah (Luke 1:70). These uses clearly speak of persons dedicated to the service of God, recognized as specially belonging to God and impelled by the Holy Spirit.

*The Holy Spirit.* By far the most common use of holiness language in the Gospels, though, is in reference to God's *Holy* Spirit. As in the Old Testament, the adjective "holy" marks this Spirit as an expression of the one creator God, unique among whatever other "spirits" there are. This Spirit crafted Jesus' human body (Matt. 1:18; Luke 1:35), revealed him publicly as Messiah at his baptism (Luke 3:22; John 1:33), and accompanied him in doing sign-miracles (Matt. 12:28).

The gospel of John especially emphasizes Jesus as bringer of the Spirit, as a result of his forthcoming death and resurrection (for example, John 4:10–14, 23–24; 7:37–39; 14:15–17, 26; 20:21–22). To a lesser extent, Luke does this also, though this theme is more prominent in Acts (Luke 24:49; Acts 2:32–33, 38).

Why are we now talking about the Spirit instead of about holiness? Because if we were to read the New Testament as a first-century Jewish person would have heard it, we automatically would connect in our minds the themes of the *coming of the Spirit* and the *holiness of God's people*. The Old Testament prophesied a future giving of the Spirit to Israel that would lead to God's people being cleansed and reconsecrated to him, and which would lead them to fulfill God's will (Ezek. 36:22–28). Jesus probably was alluding to this prophecy when he taught his disciples to pray, "Hallowed be your name" (Matt. 6:9). We could translate this as well, "Cause your name to be sanctified."

Jesus lived so completely and obviously in the Spirit's presence, was so perfectly the expression of God's presence in the flesh, that demons in terror acclaimed him "the Holy One of God" (Mark 1:24; Luke 4:34). He is not *a* holy man but "the Holy One of Israel" (see Isa. 1:4).

Here we see a common theme in New Testament teaching about Jesus: He is *like* great servants of God in the past, but *greater than* them. Jesus was the one "sanctified" by the Father and sent into the world (John 10:36), so much a "part" of God that he could say, "Anyone who has seen me has seen the Father" (14:9). His holiness was expressed in living out God's character so powerfully that his earthly life was sinless; he challenged his opponents, with confidence, to find any wrongdoing in his life at all (8:46).

Jesus teaches his followers to pray that God's name "be made holy." Since Scripture does not portray humans as causing God to be holy, some understand this petition as asking that God's name be "revered" by the whole earth—that God's self be regarded as holy, that God's name, his reputation, be treated with the awe it deserves. In this sense, it would reflect Paul's picture of the whole creation bowing in reverence to Jesus and in glorification of God the Father (Phil. 2:10–11). Others take this petition essentially as asking for God to wrap up history, to vindicate his "name" before all sentient beings by his awesome epiphany on the day of judgment. The goal of history and of prayer is that all humanity acknowledge the true God—Father, Son, and Spirit—as holy.

*The Gospel of John.* John's gospel tells us Jesus prayed for his disciples' sanctification (17:17–19). The context suggests this happens in two ways: by the Father's *truth*, which the Son has revealed to them according to his commission; and by the Son's perfect obedience to the Father, described as his sanctifying himself (17:19). Jesus set the pattern for his disciples, even though as a model he far transcends those called to be like him. He described himself as "sanctified" and "sent into the world" (10:36), just as later he would pray for his disciples to be sanctified, then announce they, too, would be sent into the world (17:17; 20:21). Immediately after this announcement of their sending, Jesus bestowed the Holy Spirit on them and spoke about forgiveness of sins (20:22–23).

Thus we see that for John, sanctification has to do with *believers' calling from God and the divine purpose* or, in other words, with "mission." We are not sanctified to be hid in a corner and preserved from trouble or temptation; we are not cosmic china cups on display. Jesus never prayed that God take his disciples out of the world, but that we stand successfully in it as a lighthouse pointing to God.

Sanctification also is associated with the coming of the *Spirit*, for multiple reasons. For one, Jesus' coming made possible the new covenant God had promised to Israel. A large part of this promise was that God would come to live with and in his people in a new way, leading them to be devoted to him and to want to please him by keeping his law—to be made holy, to be *sanctified* (compare Ezek. 36:24–27 with John 4:21–24). The Spirit empowers God's people by communicating God's holiness and assisting them both to desire and do his will.

Sanctification also is associated with the Spirit because as a "part" of who God is, the Spirit is *holy* and therefore brings holiness to those in whom he lives. This holiness, like the Spirit himself, is a *gift* to the believer, presented as part of God's plan, by means of Jesus who died and rose again to accomplish this for us. Notice Jesus prayed for the *Father* to sanctify his disciples; he did not ask the disciples (in this context) to sanctify themselves (John 17:17).

This prayer of John 17 also speaks to us of a common theme of New Testament theology: that believers participate in the life and existence of Jesus and share in his benefits. Thus, what Jesus possesses is extended to us both now and in the future (see Rom. 6:1–5; 1 Cor. 15:22). The prayer of Jesus in John 17 is really another way of stating the reality of John 15:1–11, that Jesus is the "vine" and those who believe in him and God are "branches," deriving our identity and life from the vine. Since Jesus is holy, Spirit-endowed, and sent into the world by the Father to witness to God's love, there is no way his disciples can be anything other than also holy, Spirit-endowed, and sent into the world to witness to God's love.

*The Synoptic Gospels.* Though the other gospels do not use this "sanctification" terminology, we can see similar ideas there, once we know how to recognize them. For instance, the call to total commitment to God and his kingdom, valuing it above all earthly possessions, honors, family, or even one's own life, is a call to be God's holy people (see Matt. 6:25–33; Luke 12:22–31). When Jesus made "unclean" people clean, it was a sign that *Jesus is the one who bestows holiness*: Peter (a sinner, Luke 5:8); a leper (Luke 5:12–13); tax collectors and "sinners" (Luke 5:27–32); Gentiles (Mark 7:24–30; Luke 7:2–10); a corpse (you can't get more unclean than that! Mark 5:22–23, 35–43; Luke 7:11–16); a prostitute (Luke 7:36–50); a woman with a hemorrhage, which made her ceremonially unclean, an "untouchable" (Mark 5:24–34).

Jesus' audience understood these healings not only as a matter of health, but also of the individual being brought from outside society to inside, from unclean to clean, from being banned from Temple worship to being qualified to enter God's holy courts. The physical gift of healing in these people's lives was an acted-out transformation of their status. This shocked some leaders more than anything else Jesus did, that he had the audacity to say the unclean were clean, that sinners could be God's holy people, fully part of true Israel. Yet Scripture declares that an Israelite who was "clean" was, *by definition*, God's holy person.

## THE BOOK OF ACTS

Acts tells how the Church expanded, due to the presence and activity of the Holy Spirit. The gift and empowerment of the Spirit made the mission of the early church both possible and successful (Acts 1:5, 8; 2:1–4); the Spirit was given to all who acknowledged Jesus as Lord and God's Messiah. The outpouring of the Spirit was the mark that the age of fulfilled prophecy had arrived (Acts 2:33, 38; 10:44; 11:15–17). Those who believed—both Jew and Gentile—are labeled "saints" (Acts 9:13, 32, 41; 26:10), and "those who are sanctified"—literally, the "made-holy-ones" (Acts 20:32; 26:18).

It is hard not to suspect a connection between these facts: that the *Holy* Spirit creates a church of *holy* ones, and that this is all possible because of what Jesus, the *holy* servant of God, did for humanity in his life, death, and resurrection (Acts 3:14; 4:27, 30). When we add the cultural context of first-century Judaism and see the echoes of Old Testament Israel as God's *holy* nation, it is even clearer.

## THE LETTERS OF PAUL

Paul considered *all* Christians to be "holy" to God (saints) because they belong to God; They have been purchased with Christ's death on the cross (Rom. 6:22; 1 Cor. 6:19–20; Col. 1:22). It is curious that Paul wrote a great deal about holiness to the one church that appears least holy in all his letters—Corinth! They were "called to be saints" (1 Cor. 1:2; literally, this is "called saints," that is, designated as saints); they were to participate in service to other saints (16:1, 15; 2 Cor. 8:4; 9:1). The sign that they belonged to God was the presence of the Holy Spirit within them, sometimes called God's "seal" or mark of ownership (2 Cor. 1:21–22; Eph. 1:13). Collectively they were God's holy temple (1 Cor. 3:16–17). This holiness, or sanctification, is given "in Christ Jesus" as a divine act of grace to those who are believers (1:2; 6:11).

Does this mean the story of holiness ends with the confession of faith, "Jesus is Lord" (1 Cor. 12:3), and nothing more needs to be done? Although in some texts Paul speaks as though Christians *already* are holy people as soon as they are saved, in others he speaks as though *becoming holy* or *continuing in holiness* is the duty of a Christian. Paul chastised the Corinthians for carrying on in many ways that were inconsistent with their identity in Christ, and asked them to change their behavior (1 Cor. 1:10–13; 5:1–2, 11–13; 6:15–20). He even spoke of their "completing" (Greek *epiteleō*) the holiness God had given them: "Let us purify ourselves from everything that contaminates body and spirit, perfecting holiness out of reverence for God" (2 Cor. 7:1 TNIV).

Paul also encouraged the Thessalonian church to put into practice the holiness they already were called to, especially in the area of sexual purity (1 Thess. 4:1–7). Christians must make a decision to "present your members as slaves to righteousness for sanctification," Paul told the Romans (Rom. 6:19 NRSV). In these texts Paul seems to have regarded

sanctification as something one must enter into with a sense of willing participation, not as a mere passive recipient. Indeed, if taken out of context, one would be tempted to say these texts present sanctification as a purely human achievement. That is not really Paul's view, of course, but I mention it to underline how strongly the element of synergism—humans working together with God—comes to the fore in these texts.

This evidence reveals a paradox well known to scholars of Paul, sometimes summed up in the slogan "Become what you are." On the one hand, sanctification is an act of God, obtained by faith on the basis of what Jesus did for us. On the other hand, it is something we are called to enter into, preserve, and continue to live in by our own choice. How can both be true? One answer is to think of salvation and sanctification, not as though they were concrete possessions like a new coffeemaker, but instead as new relationships we are called into by God's grace. As a relationship, it is already present, but it is, as well, something we need to work on. It is both a gift and a calling.

On the day a child is born, two persons automatically become that child's mother and father as a biological fact. Yet we all know that to be a good parent, one must choose to embrace that role and practice it. On the other hand, it is possible to be a bad parent, a neglectful parent, or even a parent who abandons his or her children. The biological fact of birth does not mean we have fulfilled what God calls us to be as parents.

So it is with sanctification. We are reborn into God's family as holy people due to the death and resurrection of Jesus on our behalf. But that is neither the end of the story, nor all there is to say about holiness. Holiness, too, must be embraced. It must be practiced. Otherwise, we risk losing what is ours by right. This is where the role of the Holy Spirit comes in. Paul said we are too weak to fight sin on our own (Rom. 7:7–25). The Spirit is given to every believer as an ally in the fight against sin and selfishness (8:9–14). As Paul put it, the Spirit opposes "the flesh" (Gal. 5:16–18).

One of Paul's letters gives a name to the Wesleyan concept of "entire sanctification." In 1 Thessalonians 5:23 (NRSV), Paul prayed, "May the God of peace himself sanctify you entirely; and may your spirit and soul and body be kept sound and blameless at the coming of our Lord Jesus Christ." The word translated "entirely" signals a wish that Christians be "completely" sanctified in every aspect of their lives, or perhaps that the work of sanctifying be brought to a perfect finish. The fact that Paul prayed for this suggests he may have believed the process of sanctification was incomplete. Both the goal and the motive for sanctification is that when Jesus returns we may greet him as Savior, rather than as Judge. By the grace of his work on our behalf, and by our faith-lives that accept and act out this grace, we may be regarded as "blameless" by the Father's love.

In my opinion, nowhere does the New Testament explicitly address the question whether sanctification is "instantaneous" or "gradual." That may be a legitimate question to ask today, but I am not sure it was a question Paul or Jesus asked or answered. Rather, sanctification is presented, I believe, as part of the life journey of a disciple. To ask Paul, "When are we perfectly sanctified?" is like asking, "When have I perfectly loved my spouse?" The answer is that it is something that happens every day as God works in us and we work with God.

## THE GENERAL/CATHOLIC EPISTLES

The book of Hebrews stresses the link between Jesus' death and our being made holy. Much more than John, and even more than Paul, it emphasizes that Jesus' death is *sacrificial.* In fulfillment of the Old Testament sacrifices, the Son offered himself in accordance with God's plan, which achieved our sanctification (10:10–14; 13:12). The holiness of God's people is based not on our achievement, but on Christ's.

Nevertheless, one can sin even against one's own holy nature and alienate oneself from God. In Hebrews, the great threat to Christians is apostasy. In a time of suffering and persecution, believers were tempted to deny publicly that they believed Jesus to be God's Son, and to take refuge in claiming to be Jewish instead. Judaism was a protected religion in the Roman Empire; Christianity was not. The book of Hebrews stresses that since believers are sanctified to God and to his service (2:11; 13:1–16), they (and we) ought not do anything inconsistent with our identity, and especially ought we to be ready to suffer for him. To deny Jesus would be to reject the very basis of our own holiness, and therefore to reject belonging to God (10:26–31).

The same duality we found in Paul—that holiness is both a gift from God and something Christians must decide to work at—is prominent in 1 Peter also. Christians are sanctified by the Holy Spirit and, therefore, are a "holy people" (1:2; 2:9); yet, we are instructed to live out that holiness. Peter does not give much specific detail on what this holy living is, though he does mention purging hatred, envy, and malicious talk (2:1), generally avoiding sinful excesses (4:1–5), practicing humility (3:8; 5:5–6), and being ready to suffer for Christ (3:9, 14–17; 4:1–2).

John's first epistle does not use the vocabulary of holiness we see elsewhere; nevertheless, Wesleyans traditionally have understood this letter as supplying important insights into the holiness of God's people. First, this letter strongly argues that persons who believe Jesus is God's Son are "born of God" and abide in him ("positional holiness": 1 John 2:23–24; 4:15; 5:1). We then are instructed to live in love and righteousness ("lived-out holiness": 3:4–11; 4:11–12; 5:1–2, and throughout the letter), so that these two naturally go together.

Second, this letter declares it the aim of Christian living to be without sin (2:1; 3:6), for John portrays spiritual realities in black and white terms: either one is living with God or not; either one is in sin or not; either one keeps God's commandment to love or not. God does not sin, and God's people do not sin. At 3:3 (NRSV), the letter uses two very rare words for holiness or purity before God. John first tells his readers that, as God's children, Christians have a future promised them in which God will reveal himself to them fully, and they will be like him. Then he says, "And all who have this hope in him purify themselves, just as he is pure [or "holy"]." John Wesley depended heavily on statements in 1 John for his arguments about sanctification in *A Plain Account of Christian Perfection.*

Third, 1 John is important because it ties together right living with loving (for instance, 1 John 2:5, 7–11; 3:11–18, 23; 4:16–21). Again, this was important for Wesley, who correctly saw that the ideal of perfection in the New Testament is not merely abstaining from everything bad, but perfectly loving as God loves (see Matt. 5:43–48; Mark 12:28–31). This returns us to that central motif of Jesus' teaching, that love of God and love of neighbor are the greatest commandments and take us closest to the heart of God.

## THE BOOK OF REVELATION

Finally, the book of Revelation has some significant things to say about holiness. In a striking intertextual echo, John envisioned the throne of God at the end of time; there, God's servants surround him with cries of "Holy," just as in Isaiah's vision (Rev. 4:8; Isa. 6:1–3). This holy God ultimately will vindicate his name, his Messiah, and his people who are consecrated to him. He will punish evil and resurrect his saints. God will not permit anything "unclean" (the opposite of holy) to dwell with his resurrected people (Rev. 21:27). God will summon a *holy* city in which God's *holy* people will live in peace and joy with him forever (21:2, 10, 27; 22:11).

## IN CONCLUSION

Jesus carried forward the view of the Old Testament, that God's people are to be consecrated to him, and in belonging to God are to reflect his nature in their lives.

Both Paul and the writer to the Hebrews reflected on how Jesus' death fulfilled all the Old Testament had looked forward to in its sacrificial system. Jesus' death and resurrection are the grounds for making believers holy, as a gift to those who have faith in God and in the Son he sent. That gift-holiness is to be turned into lived-holiness, with the aid of the Spirit.

Love is key to understanding this lived-out holiness, something Paul says indirectly, and 1 John tells us quite clearly. Holy people love their neighbors in proportion to their faith in God. This love ought to be given especially to fellow believers, but ultimately even to enemies, as Jesus taught. Revelation reminds us that God has a goal in mind for the world and especially for those who love him; that goal involves a life with God that follows and transcends death, a holy existence in a holy place in which believers joyfully and fully belong to God.

## ACTION/REFLECTION SUGGESTIONS

**1.** Do you tend to think of sanctification more as *gift* or as *achievement*? How about your congregation? If there is an over-balance on one side, what could be done to correct this?

**2.** For one week, think deliberately about your body as something holy to God. Ask yourself what *God's* body ought to be fed, what it ought to drink, how it should exercise or care for itself, how it should be used in relation to others.

**3.** Meditate on the trait of humility, which Jesus associated with being holy, and which 1 Peter does also. It may mean speaking less about yourself, becoming less critical, or pushing yourself to find good things to praise and acknowledge about others. It may mean something different for you, but it should mean *something*.

**4.** If holiness and love go together, does this mean practicing love is also practicing holiness?

4

# JOHN AND CHARLES WESLEY ON SANCTIFICATION

*John R. Tyson*

*Jesus said, "You, therefore, must be perfect,*
*as your heavenly Father is perfect."*

—Matthew 5:48

*This doctrine [Christian perfection] is the grand depositum which God has lodged with the people called Methodists; and for the sake of propagating this chiefly He appeared to have raised us up.*

—John Wesley

As we investigate John and Charles Wesley's understanding of sanctification, "a holiness of heart and life," we have an opportunity to examine the theological construct generally considered to be Methodism's most distinctive doctrine. This certainly was John's viewpoint, as the quotation above illustrates. In looking at this particular issue, Charles is seen both as a constant collaborator with his brother and as a unique contributor in his own right to the Wesleys' most distinctive doctrine.

## THE EARLY YEARS: EPWORTH AND OXFORD

In tracing the development of the Wesleys' understanding of sanctification, we have to begin at the Epworth manse, where they imbibed a unique blend of Anglican spirituality and Puritan piety. Both their father, Samuel, and their mother, Susanna, had been converts to the Church of England. While their father taught them theology and philosophy, in their mother the boys met a Christian spirituality associated with personal devotion and the examination of one's conscience. Hence, at college, both John and Charles wrote to their father when they had questions about theology, but they wrote to their mother about their devotional life and spiritual struggles.

The paper trail for tracing the development of the Wesleys' understanding of sanctification becomes clearer as we move to their collegiate years at Oxford University. In 1729, Charles recalled that he and a few of his fellow students had earned themselves the "harmless name of Methodists" by attending the weekly Eucharist and following "the method of study prescribed by the University."[1] This small group of devout and earnest college students became, under John's direction, the Oxford Holy Club. It was typical of their complementary strengths that the friendliness and buoyant personality of Charles got the group started and John's organizational genius gave it shape and direction.

Their reading of the Greek New Testament and the church fathers set the Oxford Methodists on a regimen of spiritual disciplines aimed at producing holiness of heart and life. They devoured devotional classics such as Kempis's *Imitation of Christ*, as well as more contemporary works such as Jeremy Taylor's *Holy Living and Holy Dying* and *A Serious Call to a Devout and Holy Life* by William Law. John Wesley reported that in 1726 he read Kempis's "Christian Pattern"; it taught him "the nature and extent of inward religion," hence, "the religion of the heart now appeared to me in a stronger light than ever it had done before."[2]

The Oxford Methodists not only read these books, they emulated their doctrine and practices. In 1729 Charles read Henry Scougal's devotional work *The Life of God in the Soul of Man*. He subsequently loaned the book to fellow Holy Club member George Whitefield, and it became the instrument of Whitefield's evangelical conversion. In that book, Charles met with what would be his fundamental definition of the goal and the nature of sanctification, as Scougal urged: A true religion is a union of the soul with God, a real participation in the divine nature, the image of God drawn upon the soul, or in the apostle's phrase, "it is Christ formed within us."

The Oxford Methodists also read William Law's *Practical Treatise on Christian Perfection*. John intimated that Law's treatise "convinced me more than ever, of the absolute impossibility of being half a Christian." Law's work also gave the Methodists the impetus to strive for Christian perfection, as "the very height of holiness and purity." Law defined perfection as a "regular draught of holy tempers" (attitudes), which made it clear he was not simply giving a discourse on moral action (as was so often the case in contemporary Anglicanism).[3] For Law, as for the Wesleys, Christian perfection amounted to an utter transformation of the inner person. From William Law, the Wesleys gained a vision of holiness and Christian perfection that would become their guiding aim for the rest of their lives.

Their reading of the New Testament also profoundly shaped the Wesleys' understanding of sanctification as Christian perfection. "In the year 1729," John Wesley wrote, "I began not only to read but to study the Bible as the one, the only standard of truth, and pure religion." In doing so, the Wesleys came to see that "conformity to the Master" was the essential nature of true Christianity.[4]

On January 1, 1733, it was John Wesley's turn, as a fellow of Lincoln College, to preach "before the university" at St. Mary's Church, Oxford. In the sermon he preached, "The Circumcision of the Heart,"[5] he gave a classic definition of Christian perfection as a cleansing from all sin, a renewing of the inner nature, according to the image of Christ, and a filling with God's love, which fulfills all the requirements of God's law. The inner "circumcision of the heart" John described as

> that habitual disposition of soul which, in the sacred writings, is termed holiness; and which directly implies the being cleansed from sin, "from all filthiness both of flesh and spirit"; and by consequence, the being endued with those virtues which were in Christ Jesus; the being so "renewed in the image of our mind," as to be "perfect as our Father in heaven is perfect."[6]

That this was a "perfection" in and through love was also made clear in this same sermon: "If there be any virtue, if there be any praise, they are all comprised in this one word—love. In this is perfection and glory and happiness."[7]

"Circumcision of the heart" John Wesley also equated with having all one's life and attention centered upon God; he called this unity of focus and motives "the one thing needful." He urged, "Have no end, no ultimate end, but God. Thus our Lord: 'One thing is needful.' And if thine eye be singly fixed on this one thing, 'thy whole body shall be full of light.'"[8]

## SHARED EARLY SERMONS

In October 1735, the Wesley brothers found themselves on board *The Simmonds*, headed for the New World. Charles was assigned to rough duty as both administrative secretary and pastor in the primitive military outpost on St. Simons Island, Frederica. John served as parish pastor in infant Georgia's only city, Savannah. Both while on *The Simmonds* heading toward Georgia and on *The London Galley* headed to Boston on the first leg of his return trip, Charles busied himself making copies of several of his brother's sermons; while these sermons were composed by John, they were preached by Charles.[9] This event gives particular insight into the depth of their partnership in ministry; it also gives us abundant witness to their shared understanding of sanctification.

While several of these sermons bear upon the Wesleys' doctrine of sanctification, two in particular merit special attention. The first, "The Single Eye," is based on Matthew 6:22–23 (KJV): "The light of the body is the eye; if therefore thine eye be single, thy whole body shall be full of light. But if thine eye be evil, thy whole body shall be full of darkness." Composed by John and copied by Charles from John's manuscript, the sermon was preached by Charles Wesley both in America and in England, and both before and after his conversion experience.

The sermon is about purity of intention, which was to be found through a person's heart not being "divided between two ends; if in all thy thoughts, words, and works thou hast only one view, namely to serve and please God: 'thy whole body shall be full of light.'" This is the light that shines upon the way to sanctification; as Wesley wrote, "This single intention will be a light in all thy paths; all darkness and doubt will vanish before it. All will be plain before thy face. Thou wilt clearly see the way wherein thou shouldst go, and steadily walk in it." Contrariwise, Wesley wrote, "If thou aimest at anything besides *the one thing needful*, namely a recovery of the image of God; 'thy whole body shall be full of darkness;' thou wilt see no light, which way so ever thou turnest."[10]

The aforementioned phrase, "the one thing needful," is the title of another early sermon that has significant bearing upon the Wesleys' understanding of sanctification. It was based on Luke 10:42 (KJV), in which Jesus said, "But one thing is needful: and Mary hath chosen that good part, which shall not be taken away from her." Charles also preached this sermon both before and after his conversion experience, and both he and John continued to use the phrase "the one thing needful" as an important metaphor for purity of heart and the recovery of the image of God within a person.

Charles, in particular, considered entire sanctification or Christian perfection to be the recovery of the image of God, in which all humans had been created. This was an utterly unqualified conception of perfection, which amounted to the "original righteousness" in which humans had been created before the fall into sin. Charles preached in this sermon, "To recover our first estate, from which we are thus fallen, is the one thing now needful; to re-exchange the image of Satan for the image of God, bondage for freedom, sickness for health. Our one great business is to raise out of our souls the likeness of our destroyer, and to be born again, to be formed anew after the likeness of our Creator."[11] Since love is both the image and the nature of God, an infusion of God's love is able to transform the human soul into its original, pristine state. "Love is the health of the soul," Wesley wrote, "the full exertion of all its power, the perfection of all its faculties. Therefore, since the enjoyment of these was the one end of our creation, the recovery of them is the one thing needful."[12] In Charles's holiness parlance, sanctification is "the one thing needful," a restoration of the image of God within, which becomes practicable when "the one thing needful" becomes the object of our complete focus and intention—that is to say, when it becomes "the single eye."

## CHARLES AND JOHN'S EVANGELICAL CONVERSIONS

In May 1738, after the depressing failure of their Georgia mission, both the Wesleys experienced dramatic evangelical conversions; Charles's came on May 21, and John's on May 24. We have already seen, however, that they had been preaching and striving for holiness of heart and life long before those dramatic events. One of the important transitions that occurred in their conversions was that the Wesleys accepted the Reformation doctrine of justification by faith alone and distinguished more decisively between justification and sanctification.

Three months after his conversion, Charles described this development to his former mentor, William Law. "I told him," Charles wrote in his journal, "he was my schoolmaster to bring me to Christ; but the reason why I did not come sooner to Him, was, my seeking to be sanctified before I was justified."[13] Fully characteristic of the Wesley brothers was the fact that they soon became mass evangelists who preached outdoors to multitudes of people. They also published an important book that reflected their newfound faith and the reorientation of their doctrines of justification and sanctification. Somewhat surprising, however, is the fact that the book was a hymnal! In the preface to *Hymns and Sacred Poems* (1739), they reported they had leaned too heavily upon the work of Christian mystics, which had produced confusion in their earlier understanding of the role of sanctification. They wrote, "The sole cause of our acceptance with God . . . is the righteousness and death of Christ, who fulfilled God's law, and died in our stead. And even the condition of it is not (as they suppose) our holiness either of heart or life; but our faith alone."[14]

This same preface evidences a second important development; it shows *how* the Wesleys had come to understand the way a person receives Christian perfection. Focusing their attention on Acts 2, they considered it "the gift of the Holy Spirit," which was directly connected to the first disciples' "'fellowship and in breaking of bread,' and in praying [together] in one accord [Acts 2:41–42]." This taught them that sanctification is learned in the context of small groups, and through faith-filled attention to spiritual disciplines.

The Wesleys soon required that those who had been converted through their evangelism, and who wanted to be "Methodist," must become members both of a Methodist Society and of a class meeting. The "Rules of the United Societies" (1739) urged the members to "'flee from the wrath to come' [Matt. 3:7], to be saved from their sins." To that end Methodists promised, first, to "do no harm," such as swearing, breaking the Sabbath, drunkenness, buying or selling liquors, brawling, and so forth; secondly, to "[do] good," both to the bodies and to the souls of their neighbors, by "giving food to the hungry, by clothing the naked, by visiting or helping them that are sick or in prison," and by "instructing, reproving or exhorting" all with whom they had connection, to the good of their souls.

The third promise of the "Rules" was "to attend upon all the ordinances of God." These "ordinances," or spiritual disciplines, included "the public worship of God; the ministry of the word, either read or expounded; the supper of the Lord; family and private prayer; searching the Scriptures; and fasting or abstinence."[15] Hence, their preface concluded, "The gospel of Christ knows of no religion, but social; no holiness but social holiness. 'Faith working by love' is the length and breadth and depth and height of Christian Perfection."[16]

## CHARLES WESLEY'S EARLY HYMNS

Almost immediately after his conversion experience, Charles wrote a hymn to express his newfound faith. In fact, he wrote several hymns over the next few days, and when John visited him, fresh from his Aldersgate experience, they sang Charles's hymns together. These were among the first of Charles's more than nine thousand hymns and sacred poems, and they offer us a window into his heart and mind.

One of the hymns Charles wrote immediately after his conversion experience was published in the 1739 hymnal under the title "Free Grace." It is more familiar to us by its first line: "And can it be, that I should gain." The first few verses express the wonder and excitement Charles found in God's grace made available to him in Christ: "Amazing love! How can it be / That Thou, my God, shouldst die for me?" Stanzas 4 and 5 are replete with what would become standard Wesleyan salvation themes. The life of sin is likened to a sinful slumber. Justification by faith leads directly to deliverance from sin and to new birth—which in Wesleyan parlance often is called initial sanctification. Deliverance from sin brings with it the witness of the Spirit ("the still small voice"), as Christ is formed within the Christian by faith:

4. Long my imprison'd spirit lay
Fast bound in sin and nature's night:
Thine eye diffused a quickening ray;
I woke; the dungeon flamed with light;
My chains fell off, my heart was free,
I rose, went forth, and follow'd Thee.

5. Still the small inward voice I hear,
That whispers all my sins forgiven;
Still the atoning blood is near,
That quench'd the wrath of hostile Heaven:
I feel the life His wounds impart;
I feel my Saviour in my heart.[17]

A year after his conversion, Charles Wesley penned a long hymn (eighteen verses) that he titled "For the Anniversary Day of One's Conversion." One could argue it has become his most famous hymn; certainly, it is one of Christianity's most famous conversion hymns. John, who was Charles's editor, shortened it to eight verses by omitting some of his original stanzas and doubling up the others. The modern version begins with Charles's original verse 7: "O for a thousand tongues to sing." This verse emerges from the poet's praise for the conversion he already had celebrated in verses 1 through 6.

Several of Charles's original verses carry references to sanctification. For example, the first line of verse 10 reminds us that Jesus "breaks the power of cancell'd sin, / He sets the prisoner free." This subtle reference affirms both that sin is cancelled (by justification) and that sin has no hold over the redeemed Christian (sanctification); such a person certainly is "set free."

## CLASSICAL EXPRESSIONS OF CHRISTIAN PERFECTION

In the 1740s, the Wesleyan doctrine of sanctification reached many of its classical expressions. John had begun preaching a perfection of heart and mind that was, nonetheless (to borrow the phrase of his critics), an "*imperfect* perfection." His preaching was based in his definition of sin as "a *voluntary* transgression of a *known* law of God." First voiced in his sermon on 1 John 3:9—"Whosoever is born of God doth not commit sin"—John's definition of sin focuses our attention on what a person wills and knows, and hence on one's heart and mind, not on one's performance. The inner reservoir of a person's identity can be transformed by the Holy Spirit and the in-flowing of divine love, yet this does not rule out the possibility that a person may "error" in many ways.

This, then, is a volitional perfection, or wholeness, in which a person learns to love and follow God's will, yet which makes no claims about the utter perfection that belongs only to the glory of God. Hence, a believer can mirror the will and law of God without becoming divine, or perfect, in every sort of performance or aspect. John Wesley's insightful definition appears first in his Standard Sermon number 19, which he preached as early as September 23, 1739, and January 17, 1740.[18] He proclaimed,

> By "sin" I here understand outward sin, according to the plain, common acceptation of the word: an actual, voluntary transgression of the law; of the revealed, written law of God; of any commandment of God acknowledged to be such at the time that it is transgressed. But "whosoever is born of God," while he abideth in faith and love and in the spirit of prayer and thanksgiving, not only "doth not," but "cannot" thus "commit sin."[19]

This definition became the lynch-pin of his argument in his famous *Plain Account of Christian Perfection* and resounded all across the broad span of his ministry. This qualified definition of sin meant the Wesleys could claim victory over willful and voluntary sin, without claiming to be utterly sinless in the same sense that God is utterly free from sin and error. While Christians may live free from willful sin, because of the transformation of their hearts and minds, they will continue to make "mistakes." These mistakes or errors are not properly called "sins" because they are done without the knowledge and the will of the person, yet they are still transgressions of God's law.

## DISCUSSIONS IN THE ANNUAL CONFERENCES

The doctrine of Christian perfection frequently was a matter of conversation at the annual conferences the Wesleys held with their preachers. In 1744, the annual conference was held at Wesley's London Foundry; the "Minutes of Conference" indicate that sanctification and Christian perfection were hot topics. Written in a question and answer format, the "Minutes" began the process of defining the Wesleyan conception of sanctification as Christian perfection:

Q1. What is it to be sanctified?
A. To be renewed in the image of God, in righteousness and true holiness.

Q3. What is implied in being a perfect Christian?
A. The loving the Lord our God with all our heart, and with all our mind, and soul (Deut. 6:5).[20]

This discussion continued at the next annual conference, in August 1745, held at the Wesleys' New Room, in Bristol. The minutes suggest that questions were arising among the Methodists about the timing of Christian perfection, or "entire sanctification." There seems to have been agreement that this work of the Holy Spirit breaks the power of original sin in a person's life, and he or she is sanctified in body, mind, and soul. The minutes allow that entire sanctification generally occurs "a little before death," but they also seem to chide those who assume it can occur *no sooner* than death. Sanctification as it related to the "article of death" continued to be a matter of controversy among the early Methodists. Subsequently, in 1747, Charles published what would become one of his most famous hymns on Christian perfection: "Love Divine,

All Loves Excelling." In the first verse of the hymn, Jesus is presented as love personified. Salvation is ours, when Jesus dwells in "every trembling heart":

1. Love divine, all loves excelling,
Joy of heaven, to earth come down,
Fix in us Thy humble dwelling,
All Thy faithful mercies crown!
Jesus, Thou art all compassion,
Pure, unbounded love Thou art;
Visit us with Thy salvation!
Enter every trembling heart.

The love Jesus incarnates in the believer's heart is none other than God's perfecting love. It turns the singer into God's "new creation"; what had been lost in sin is "perfectly restored" as the singer is "changed from glory into glory" (verse 3) and prepared to enter heaven, and an eternity in God's presence.

## *SHORT HYMNS ON SELECT PASSAGES OF SCRIPTURE*

In 1762, Charles published *Short Hymns on Select Passages of Scripture.* In the preface, Charles indicated he intended to address the topic of Christian perfection in these hymns. "Several of the hymns," he wrote, "are intended to prove, and several to guard, the doctrines of Christian Perfection; I durst not publish the one without the other." Charles admitted he was using strong language to chastise "Enthusiasts and Antinomians, who not living up to their profession, give abundant occasion to them that seek it, and cause the truth to be evil spoken of."

In Charles's *Short Hymns* his own distinctive emphases on Christian perfection came to the forefront. These are easily traced, since John did not see the manuscript prior to publication, and subsequently annotated it with comments about hymns he did not like. Three specific questions emerged between the Wesley brothers on the topic of Christian perfection: (1) Was Charles setting the doctrine of Perfection too high? (2) Is Christian perfection an instantaneous blessing or is it received gradually—as Charles stressed—over the course of an entire life? (3) Does it occur, as Charles's later hymns imply, "in the article of death," that is, just before a person's death? Charles's *Short Hymns* show that he tended to take the opposite emphasis from that of his brother on all three of these questions.[21]

## THE DEFINITIVE *PLAIN ACCOUNT*

In 1777, John Wesley republished *A Plain Account of Christian Perfection*, his definitive work on the subject. It was designed to explain the Wesleyans' most distinctive doctrine, to show that the Wesleys were in substantial agreement on the doctrine, and to show that he had not changed his views on Christian perfection since 1725. The treatise concludes with an itemized eleven-point summary of their views. Among the important summary statements are these:

1. There is such a thing as perfection; for it is again and again mentioned in Scripture.
2. It is not so early as justification; for justified persons are to "go unto Perfection" (Heb. 6:1).
3. It is not so late as death; for St. Paul speaks of living men that were perfect (Phil. 3:15).
4. It is not absolute. Absolute perfection belongs not to man, nor to angels, But to God alone.

7. It is "perfect love" (1 John 4:18). This is the essence of it; its properties, or inseparable fruits are, rejoicing evermore, praying without ceasing, and in every thing giving thanks (1 Thess. 5:16–18).
10. It is constantly both preceded and followed by a gradual work.
11. An instantaneous change has been wrought in some believers. None can deny this.[22]

Also to be added to these statements is the Wesleys' strong awareness that true holiness is a "social holiness." It is to be sought in the context of the fellowship and accountability of a small group, in the practice of spiritual disciplines, and in the utter determination to do "all the good we can" to and for the bodies and souls of our fellow human beings.

## ACTION/REFLECTION SUGGESTIONS

**1.** Wesleyan holiness theology often is expressed in catch phrases—drawn from Scripture or from the Wesleyan tradition—that aptly describe the situation to those who understand them, but that remain unintelligible to those unfamiliar with the Wesleyan tradition. How would you explain Wesleyan phrases such as "circumcision of heart," "the one thing needful," "singleness of eye," and "Christian perfection" to someone who has not heard or read of them?

**2.** Christian Perfection, according to John and Charles Wesley, is best learned in the context of an accountability group. Why did they think this? Are you a member of a small group? If not, *why* not?

**3.** When the Wesleys urged that there is "no holiness but social holiness," they meant we need other Christians, and we need to function in the real world as a force for change and renewal. Do you "do no harm"? Do you "do all the good you can" to and for the souls and bodies of your neighbors? Do you practice "the ordinances of God" (spiritual disciplines)? How might you be more consistent and more effective with the responsibilities of "social holiness"?

## NOTES

1. John R. Tyson, ed., *Charles Wesley: A Reader* (New York: Oxford University Press, 1989), 59.

2. John Wesley, *A Plain Account of Christian Perfection* (Kansas City: Beacon Hill Press, 1966), 10.

3. Paul Stanwood, ed., *William Law* (New York: Paulist, 1978), 131.

4. Wesley, *Plain Account*, 11.

5. Albert Outler, ed., *The Works of John Wesley*, vol. I: *Sermons 1* (Nashville: Abingdon, 1984), 398–415.

6. Wesley, *Plain Account*, 12.

7. Outler, *Sermons 1*, 407.

8. Ibid., 409.

9. Richard Heitzenrater, "John Wesley's Earliest Sermons," in *Proceedings of the Wesley Historical Society*, vol. 37 (1969–70), 110–128, first drew our attention to these sermons. Kenneth G. C. Newport, ed., *The Sermons of Charles Wesley* (Oxford: Oxford University Press, 2001), gives a detailed analysis of them (74–90).

10. Kenneth G. C. Newport, ed., *The Sermons of Charles Wesley* (Oxford: Oxford University Press, 2001), 309, emphasis added.

11. Ibid., 364.

12. Ibid., 365.

13. Thomas Jackson, ed., *The Journal of Charles Wesley, A.M.,* vol. I (London: John Mason, 1840), 159.

14. Thomas Jackson, ed., *The Works of John Wesley, A.M.*, vol. XIV (London: The Wesleyan Conference, 1872), 320.

15. Jackson, *Works of John Wesley*, vol. VIII, 269–271.

16. Jackson, *Works of John Wesley*, vol. XIV, 321.

17. Tyson, *Charles Wesley: A Reader*, 103–104.

18. Outler, *Sermons 1*, 431–43.

19. Ibid., 436.

20. Jackson, *Works of John Wesley, VIII,* 279.

21. For a detailed study of the respective views of John and Charles Wesley on the matter of sanctification, see my work, *Charles Wesley on Sanctification: A Biographical and Theological Study* (Grand Rapids: Zondervan Publishing Company, 1986), republished now by Schmul Publishing Company, Salem, Ohio.

22. John Wesley, *Plain Account*, 114-115.

# THE AMERICAN SCENE

*Clarence Bence*

*That the generation to come might know, even the children yet to be born, That they may arise and tell them to their children, That they should put their confidence in God.*

—Psalm 78:6–7 (NASB)

*[God] is already renewing the face of the earth: And we have strong reason to hope that the work he hath begun, he will carry on unto the day of the Lord Jesus; that he will never intermit this blessed work of his Spirit, until he has fulfilled all his promises . . . and re-established universal holiness and happiness.*

—John Wesley

Several years ago, I returned to the holiness campground of my childhood for a Sunday morning service. The music that morning was unusually formal: we joined in singing all the stanzas of "The Church's One Foundation." We had reached the final stanza when one of those divine breakthrough moments occurred in my life, in the lines,

Yet she on earth hath union with God, the Three in One,
And mystic sweet communion with those whose rest is won.

Suddenly, all the saints who heretofore had been childhood memories of summers at this place began to fill the tabernacle: Frank Wright, the long-retired dean of Houghton College; Myrtle Lawrence, the godly pastor's wife who defined everything spiritual as "precious"; and J. Paul Hill, under whose ministry I had knelt for salvation. All were present in spirit. So were others whom I only knew from book learning—Charles Finney, Francis Asbury, and the Wesley brothers. I wept silent tears of gratitude for my godly heritage. I had been nurtured in the heart of American holiness, and I was the richer for all the influences that have shaped that tradition in the past 250 years.

## METHODIST ARRIVAL AND CAMP MEETING BEGINNINGS

The Wesleyan revival that swept England, Ireland, and Scotland was not really a holiness revival, in the sense one might use the term today. It was instead a "full salvation" revival, fueled by John Wesley's passion to see men and women saved in the broadest sense of that word. He often described his ministry as "offering Christ." He proclaimed a gospel that exalted a Savior who was able both to pardon and cleanse from sin. Although the messages that dominated his field preaching were about justification by faith, he refused to leave newly forgiven converts to struggle with their old natures and the temptation to turn back to former ways. Instead, he organized these believers into small groups, where they encouraged and admonished one another to press on to a deeper experience of sanctification, culminating in a divine assurance that they had totally died to sin and come alive in Jesus Christ. The proclamation of full salvation led to both a spiritual renewal and a moral transformation wherever the message and methods of the Wesleys spread.

However, the early Methodists arriving in America in the 1760s appear to have been Methodist in name only. Most of them were more consumed with issues of basic survival than with commitment to holy living. A group of Methodists in New York City were engaged in playing cards when one of the group, Barbara Heck, confronted them with their worldly ways. She consigned the cards and their moral behavior to fires both earthly and eternal. Her passion for holy living prompted the creation of the first organized class meeting in 1766, with the clear intent of restoring Methodism to its mission of spreading scriptural holiness throughout the land.

But American culture in the eighteenth century was not conducive to deep spirituality. Enlightenment thought had stripped Christianity of its supernatural elements, including the deity of Christ and the possibility of present-day miracles. Righteousness had been reduced to little more than common-sense morality. Independence from the King of England was far more important than submission to the King of heaven in most people's minds.

The first lay preachers, sent by Wesley to spread the revival in America, mounted horses and moved into the newly settled areas away from the seaboard cities. With Bibles and printed sermons in their saddlebags, circuit riders such as Francis Asbury and Peter Cartwright moved out into the small villages and frontier settlements of Delaware, Ohio, and Kentucky, calling men and women back to the godly heritage they had abandoned in their trek westward. Wherever the circuit riders went, they created small Methodist societies supervised by class leaders and monitored by recurring visits of traveling evangelists. While other religious groups grew incrementally with each new ship arriving from the old country, Methodism virtually exploded into the fastest-growing denomination in the newly formed United States of America.

But as Wesley had anticipated, the very success of Methodism in America led to a cooling of both its evangelistic zeal and its commitment to heart holiness. As the newly formed (1784) Methodist Episcopal Church, now independent and free from its ties to England, became more and more established in American society, its passion for a sanctifying work of grace was largely consigned to itinerant preachers who continued to call converts to entire sanctification but with diminishing results. In 1812, the denomination removed Wesley's *Plain Account of Christian Perfection* from its book of polity.

Seeds of a new movement that would revitalize the holiness message were planted in the summer of 1801, when several clergy were commissioned to travel over the Appalachian Mountains to Cane Ridge, Kentucky, to offer the sacraments of baptism and the Lord's Supper to frontier inhabitants who lacked the services of an ordained minister. Crowds grew as word spread of a great spiritual awakening at this sacramental gathering. Those who came lingered, constructing temporary dwellings that resembled military camps.

Thus, the camp meeting movement in America was born. Within a decade, numerous campgrounds with makeshift tabernacles, dining halls, and spartan cottages transformed a movement into an established institution, uniquely associated with American religion and, to a large degree, with the Holiness Movement today. Every denomination that proclaims the message of heart holiness has incorporated the camp meeting tradition into its organizational structure.

The camp meeting brought to the forefront the power of religious experience in one's personal faith. Beyond the stalwart doctrines of the church and the more traditional means of grace (prayer, Bible reading, sacraments), there always has been a deep yearning in humans for moments of divine intervention—moments so specific that one could testify with certainty that the touch from God had happened on a certain day of the week in a particular month and year. If the camp meetings provided one such opportunity for a datable experience, Charles Finney's institution of revival meetings as a structured element of religious life would bring yet another force to play on the holiness tradition in America.

## FINNEY'S REVIVALISM AND SOCIAL JUSTICE

Having experienced his own remarkable conversion from formalized religion to a deep personal relationship with God, Charles Finney began sharing a simple gospel message in homes, schoolhouses, and small churches. Before long, the impact of his messages began to electrify cities along the newly constructed Erie Canal in upstate New York.

According to Finney, these revivals were not the surprising work of God as described by Jonathan Edwards a century earlier. As a former lawyer, Finney was convinced the salvation of souls and the subsequent transformation of lives could be accomplished by a cooperative endeavor between human beings and God. He likened a revival to a crop of wheat. No farmer ever harvested the grain without the good providence of God sending sun and rain. But no farmer had a harvest worth beans without human effort and the use of the best measures available to produce the crop. Finney was convinced he had discovered the best means for generating a harvest of souls.

Chief among these "new measures" was a scheduled series of meetings specifically designated for the purpose of converting sinners and revitalizing the saints. Like any good lawyer in the courtroom, Finney would not think of ending a message without calling the congregation, his spiritual jury, to a definite verdict on the case for Christ he had just presented. He would invite those who wanted to respond affirmatively to God's call to do just that—to leave their pew and move to the front of the church, where they knelt at the communion rail or altar to settle the issue once and for all. Although Wesley's sermons had often closed with a fervent appeal to come to Christ, it was Finney who gave the altar call, as we know it, a rightful place among the essential features of the Holiness Movement for the next two centuries.

Another element of Finney's populist theology would deeply affect those Methodists who had endeavored to sustain Wesley's appeal for a sanctified life. Finney was not content with any easy believism that was simply a born-again experience without a subsequent change of life and conduct. To be a Christian was not only to trust in God's pardoning grace; it also was to obey his call to radical discipleship. For Finney, one was not simply saved from the guilt and penalty of sin; one must be converted to a transformed life.

This passion for transformation could not have happened at a more opportune moment in American religion. Two streams of thought—one secular and one theological—merged for several generations, and radically affected our national history. The secular idea was manifest destiny, a glowing optimism that this new nation, which had found independence from England, was engaged in a venture that would be unparalleled in human history. The United States could be the ideal society, governed by the people and committed to justice for all.

The theology best suited for that optimistic task was Methodist perfectionism, the confidence held by Wesley and his followers that an individual might pursue and attain a spiritual state where the inward bent to sinning was eliminated by the blood of Christ.

What was true of individual believers might be envisioned at the societal level, as well. Could not the evils of slavery and alcoholism, as well as the abuse of women and children, be eliminated by Christians united in a godly cause? In his sermon "The General Spread of the Gospel," Wesley envisioned a time when the revival that had begun in England would extend around the globe and specifically to America. The revival would go beyond spiritual awakenings to a radically reordered society where the Lord God would rule.

Thus, the three streams converged. Andrew Jackson's confidence in America's future, John Wesley's doctrine of Christian perfection spreading across the land, and Charles Finney's confidence that humans could work with God to change lives and society, combined to form a brief utopian vision that America might truly become a righteous nation. This vision soon would fade, but in that short time evangelical Christians viewed holiness as both a personal and a social experience.

In the quarter century before the American Civil War, three evangelical crusades materialized that would change the face of American culture: the abolitionist movement against slavery, the temperance/prohibitionist movement against the abuses of alcohol, and the suffrage movement that eventually would achieve equal rights for women. As both Timothy Smith and Donald Dayton have shown, these reforms were imbedded in the religious passions of those who believed righteousness exalts a nation.

But the righteous empire would not be achieved without dissension and division. The tensions within Methodism between those who were more accommodating toward culture, the slave trade in particular, and those who called for radical holiness, spawned the first denominations that would be identified distinctly as "holiness churches." The Wesleyan Methodist Connection (1843) and the Free Methodist Church (1860) were two groups who combined the teachings of Wesley on personal holiness with a passion for a godly society. The sermon delivered at the first formal ordination of a woman on American soil was preached by Luther Lee, a Wesleyan Methodist pastor and theologian. Modern-day proponents of the holiness message well could emulate the courage of social reformers such as Orange Scott, founder of the Wesleyan Methodists, and Jonathan Blanchard, first president of Wheaton College, as they applied biblical teachings of justice, mercy, and righteousness to the culture in which they lived.

## SANCTIFICATION AS A CRISIS WORK OF THE SPIRIT

Alongside this emphasis on a holy social order, other developments were working that would alter significantly the teaching of Wesley's doctrine of entire sanctification in America. Wesley had based his view of sanctification on his doctrine of the atonement—Christ's redemptive work on the cross: "The blood of Jesus Christ his Son cleanse[s] us from all sin" (1 John 1:7 KJV), and this cleansing is accomplished in the life of the believer through the work of the Holy Spirit in our lives.

But within Wesley's own lifetime, his followers began to see the Holy Spirit playing a more significant role in the sanctification of believers. Without rejecting the saving work of Christ, preachers began to speak of the Spirit, not Christ, as the Sanctifier. Scriptural support for such a view could be found in Acts, especially the second chapter, where the promise of the Father was poured out on Jesus' disciples. That baptism of the Spirit radically transformed the lives of those undergoing this Pentecostal experience, not only giving them power to witness with boldness, but as Peter reported, "he purified their hearts by faith" (Acts 15:9).

The dramatic event at Pentecost and similar outpourings of the Holy Spirit upon the early church seemed to be the perfect complement to the crisis experiences commonly associated with conversions at Finney's revivals. If an unbeliever could dramatically step from an eternal death into eternal life by an act of faith, could not one expect that the same God might sanctify the believer, who in a moment of crisis trusts him for cleansing from all sin? Would not a living sacrifice placed on the altar of consecration be entirely sanctified instantaneously as well?

Such was the contention of Phoebe Palmer and her sister, Sarah Lankford, who in 1835 began weekly prayer meetings for women (later including men) for the purpose of sharing testimonies of God's sanctifying grace and leading others into a similar experience. Palmer's view of sanctification soon became characterized as the "shorter way," in contrast to Wesley's view, which allowed for a more gradual development of virtue and growth in grace prior to an assurance of a soul cleansed of all sin. Although Wesley was persuaded that one might reach a state of "sinless" perfection in this life, he viewed it more as a goal to be pursued with all diligence because it was attainable than as an experience to be seized in a moment of conviction or intense persuasion. But the climate in American revivalism was much more conducive of a "crisis" perspective of God's saving work, and thousands of believers gave testimony of this instantaneous experience of entire sanctification.

Tuesday Meetings for the Promotion of Holiness soon spread across the eastern seaboard. Evangelists, who once called sinners to repentance during camp meetings or revival services, now offered a "second blessing": the baptism of the Holy Spirit that Christ had promised to his followers and had poured out on the day of Pentecost. This revival fervor reached its high point in the "holiness revival" of 1858. The Civil War would dampen the fires for a time, but, after the fighting had ceased, a new outbreak of religious fervor surfaced at a camp meeting in Vineland, New Jersey, in 1867. Within a short while, a resurgence of teaching on sanctification led to a renewed focus on a Christian faith that centered in religious experience more than in doctrinal precision and ecclesiastical forms. Christians who could testify of two crisis experiences—"saved and sanctified"—had discovered the secret of a happy life in God.

This revival spirit was not confined to the Methodist Church and its American branches. A flurry of new denominations emerged as this doctrine infiltrated existing churches, causing some who testified to this second blessing to leave (or be ejected) when they became vocal proponents of the doctrine. The Society of Friends (Quakers) in the Midwest divided over this issue; they remain sharply divided on the nature of salvation even today. The Church of God (Anderson) was founded in 1881 as a nondenominational holiness group.

A group of Canadian Baptists parted company with their denomination (1888) to create the Alliance of the Reformed Baptist Church, reformed by the experience of entire sanctification among its pastors and congregants. In 1892, a number of small sectarian groups joined together to form the Pilgrim Holiness Church which, along with the Reformed Baptists and Wesleyan Methodists, would merge (1968) into the present day Wesleyan Church.

The most significant clustering of holiness groups occurred in 1908, with the formation of the Pentecostal Church of the Nazarene under the leadership of Phineas Bresee and others. Centered predominantly in the Southwest in its early years, it soon spanned the continent and beyond, with holiness missions in many lands.

## PENTECOSTALISM AND DISPENSATIONALISM

But such an association with Pentecost soon proved problematic for many of the holiness denominations. In 1901, a group of students at a small Bible college in Topeka, Kansas, became convinced not only that a personal Pentecost is available to all believers, but, similarly, the miraculous sign of speaking in unknown tongues is available to believers today. In fact, they came to believe, that sign would be the incontrovertible evidence that one truly had been baptized with the Holy Spirit.

As this new Pentecostal theology spread across the land, most holiness denominations backed away from it, restricting their understanding of the work of the Holy Spirit to heart cleansing, as taught by Phoebe Palmer and the National Holiness Association, an association of holiness denominations and churches created in 1867 (and maintaining a penumbral existence today as the Christian Holiness Partnership). Although some holiness denominations like the Church of God (Cleveland, Tenn.) retained their view on sanctification and combined it with Pentecostal teaching, most became increasingly resistant to Pentecostal and charismatic practices.

That resistance was fueled in part by another movement absorbed into American religion during this same period. The teachings of John

Nelson Darby, an English Bible teacher, found fertile soil in American theology at the end of the nineteenth century. Darby had "discovered" a complex pattern of God's economy of grace—he called them dispensations—through the trajectory of human history. The pattern was always the same: a covenant between God and a select group of humans that required obedience on their part.

In each dispensation, humans eventually rejected the covenant, incurring God's wrath on the greater population. However, a remnant always was established to receive the next covenant and carry into the succeeding dispensation of grace. Darby taught that the "church age" in which we currently exist is headed toward an inevitable judgment because of modern-day human disobedience. Only a remnant of faithful Christians will be rescued from God's final outpouring of wrath in the "great tribulation." The best believers can do is to reclaim lost souls in anticipation of the impending any-moment "rapture" of the church.

Absent in this dispensational theology is any confidence that the world might be evangelized and transformed. Instead, a "lifeboat" theology developed, in which believers were called to abandon any hope that the grand ship of culture and society could be brought safely to harbor. Believers were to devote themselves unstintingly to rescuing the perishing through personal evangelism and separation from the world.

Interestingly, Darby received a cool reception to his pessimistic view of human history when he shared his views with Methodists in America!

## FUNDAMENTALIST LEAVENING

A second important feature of this dispensational view was its very literal interpretation of Christian Scripture. In such a comprehensive and complex interpretation of biblical history and prophecy, every verse took on prophetic significance. To aid the believer unskilled in the science of biblical interpretation, C. I. Scofield, another lawyer-turned-preacher, produced a study Bible (1909) with extensive notes at the bottom of each page, explaining the nuances of dispensational theology. At a time when liberal scholarship from Europe was challenging the historical veracity and theological foundations of the Scriptures, this impassioned allegiance to the literal text of the Bible was seen as the great hope of evangelical Christianity.

The Fundamentals was a series of pamphlets outlining the basic beliefs of "true Christians"—beliefs such as the deity of Christ, the bodily resurrection of the believer, the six-day creation, and Darby's views on the second coming of Christ. Their publication and free distribution, a project begun in 1909, gave rise to classic fundamentalism in America.

In the conflict over what constituted true Christianity, every believer was asked to choose this day whom they would serve—liberal or fundamentalist Christianity. As with the concurrent rise of Pentecostalism, the holiness denominations found themselves confronted by non-Wesleyan themes that held sway for a great number of evangelicals. Since the fundamentalist churches had aligned themselves against both liberal scholarship and the practice of speaking in tongues, it was almost inevitable that the holiness churches would form an uncomfortable alliance with the fundamentalist movement, even knowing full well that their views on sanctification and the attainment of holiness in this lifetime were considered heretical within the prevailing Calvinism of that camp.

The resulting influences adversely affected the Holiness Movement throughout the first half of the twentieth century. The pessimistic overtones of dispensationalism left many churches convinced that preserving their doctrine and heritage was the best option available to them. Thus, they left the path of earlier generations of holiness advocates, abandoning both a bold outreach to lost individuals and the vision of transformation of corrupt social structures.

Holiness came to be viewed, quite often, in terms of rigid legalistic practices having to do with attire and other personal behaviors. Fixing of appropriate skirt lengths for women and girls, proscription of most jewelry, and total abstinence from all tobacco, alcoholic beverages, motion pictures, and playing cards became the near-universal distinguishing marks, if not the required "evidence," of the sanctified life. The preaching of holiness, and the altar call to consecrate oneself completely to God, continued unabated in camp meetings and revival services in local churches, but the distinguishing marks of a godly life frequently were defined by the twin tests of testimonies to a crisis experience of entire sanctification and adherence to the behavioral norms just noted.

A by-product of this fundamentalist interest, and a sign of a movement coming of age, was the creation of the Wesleyan Theological Society in 1965. Here academicians from a variety of denominations affiliated with historic Methodism and the Holiness Movement met annually to probe the "fundamentals" of holiness doctrine. Significant learning was both shared and spawned at these meetings. However, one could sense the struggle to promote scholarly pursuits in a movement that was more experiential than doctrinal in its origins and activities.

## WHITHER NOW?

In the latter half of the twentieth century, a sobering phenomenon could be observed in many holiness churches. Although lip service still was given to the doctrine of entire sanctification, and candidates for ordination were thoroughly examined concerning both their understanding and their personal testimony of the baptism of the Spirit, preaching and teaching on the subject waned. While denominational leaders remained faithful to the tradition, a seeming lack of passion for the doctrine as formulated in the tradition was evident. Those who talked of the holy life moved toward more Keswickian theology, which spoke of power to live victoriously over the ever-present sinful nature, rather than of heart purity.

The Holiness Movement may have morphed into more institutional expressions, both in doctrine and structure. However, the pursuit of a vital relationship with God, manifesting itself in love of God and love of neighbor with the purity exemplified in Jesus of Nazareth, still persists. Some have endeavored to refresh the springs of holiness by more careful study of Wesley and Palmer, eliminating some of the accretions that have distorted their teachings on the subject. Others have sought to move beyond the past and create an emergent Wesleyan theology for the postmodern age.

In any case, we will not escape completely our historical ties in American religious life. In future years, the discerning historian still will find vestiges of revivalism, Pentecostalism, and fundamentalism imbedded in our teaching and practices. We may hope—we must hope—however, that the unique expression we call American holiness will continue to be the great legacy we, too, shall leave for generations to come.

## ACTION/REFLECTION SUGGESTIONS

**1.** Camp meetings and revival services in local churches have been powerfully used by God in America to "spread scriptural holiness throughout the land." Some say these methods have lost their effectiveness and should be replaced by more contemporary strategies. Recalling your own experiences or what you have heard others report, do you agree or disagree? Why or why not?

**2.** What would you consider to be the fundamental beliefs of Christianity from a Wesleyan perspective? Are you comfortable calling yourself a "Wesleyan fundamentalist"? Why or why not?

**3.** Can you think of ways our concept and experience of holiness are enriched by seeing holiness both as the work of Christ's atonement and the baptism of the Holy Spirit? What dangers might there be in focusing holiness solely on the work of one Person of the Trinity to the neglect of the others?

6

# HOLINESS IN OTHER CHRISTIAN TRADITIONS

*Richard K. Eckley*

*Therefore, since we are surrounded by such a great cloud of witnesses, let us throw off everything that hinders and the sin that so easily entangles, and let us run with perseverance the race marked out for us. Let us fix our eyes on Jesus, the author and perfecter of our faith.*

—Hebrews 12:1–2

*Holiness is not the luxury of a few. It is everyone's duty: yours and mine.*

—Mother Teresa

I had never thought the idea of ecumenical holiness to be an issue until I was confronted by a church leader outside the Houghton College campus bookstore. Waving under my nose a copy of *Five Views on Sanctification*, the text I use for teaching the doctrine of holiness in my Wesleyan Tradition course, he said, "If our professors are using texts like this, it's no wonder our pastors are messed up on our holiness theology!" He went on to assert there is only one correct view of sanctification, and "we have it."

Holiness is the concern of all the Church, not just of those of us in the tradition of the Wesleys. Though John Wesley was certainly Protestant in his understanding of salvation, he drank from all the spirited wells of Christianity, including its other two main branches—Roman Catholicism and Eastern Orthodoxy.

One of the features—for good or ill—of our present context for doing church is the public's general distrust of denominationalism and supposed doctrinal arrogance. Most churchgoers today reject the idea that any one Christian sect can corner the market on holiness or holiness teaching; as a result, they settle for a generic evangelical pabulum. The field of ecumenics offers another option, one that ecclesial bodies in the Wesleyan movement can enjoy. "Ecumenics" is from the Greek word *oikonomia*, literally, the "law of the house"; another English noun, *economics*, also stems from this Greek compound word. The economy of God's grace is found in the diverse ways the Church (corporately and individually) expresses God's activity in our lives.

By holding out the doctrine of sanctification as a key to Christian life and understanding, many of our growing churches have attracted people from diverse faith backgrounds, including those formed by the abyss of our secular culture. The call to Christlike holiness always will be a higher calling than finding one's existential purpose in today's confusing world or, even worse, merely "becoming a better you."

An obvious response to viewing the Wesleyan place in today's religious marketplace in this way is that true Christian teaching must come from Scripture alone. That usually is taken to mean there is (only) one correct way of looking at the relevant texts. However, as we have attempted to take the gospel to the entire world in this new era of global opportunity, we have come to realize that a proper biblical interpretation must take into account the unity and diversity of the entire biblical canon, while listening to the long history of the Church's use and interpretation. The Wesleyan tradition has perhaps a uniquely extended reflection on the idea of sanctification and holiness in Scripture, but we will continue to find refinement and revival in dialogue with other

Protestant, Roman Catholic, and Eastern tradition Christianities. A brief look at each will suggest some of the benefits of this exchange.

## HOLINESS FROM WITHIN PROTESTANT CHURCHES

Holiness theology almost had to force its way onto the Reformation landscape. Undoubtedly, the fear that the doctrine of sanctification would lead to some form of "self-righteousness" (perhaps even to the heresy of salvation by works) kept most sixteenth-century Protestants from entertaining any synergism between believers' faith and their good (holy) works.

Because the Wesleyan revivals began along with the rise of modernity and the Age of Reason, early dialogues with those outside the holiness tradition tended to be in some form of absolutist debates over Calvinist Reformed systems of juridical atonement. In the end, most of this discussion led to highly polarized understandings of grace and election. Most in the postmodern church find these debates tiresome and irrelevant. As Brian McLaren has pointed out, they have the tendency to compare our opponents' worst with our best.[1]

Part of the problem of proclaiming the holiness message in the current Protestant church is that our culture is not overly impressed with this kind of absolute doctrinal refinement. Some in the Wesleyan tradition have felt that if we could find some "new" way of communicating the doctrine, or could make the case better than those opposing our position, people would be convinced and would opt again for the "Wesleyan way." Holiness still is God's business, however, and no scheme or paradigm will describe completely the amazing grace bestowed on sinful humanity. Theology today looks more like the cutting of a diamond, with each Christian tradition adding a different plane of perspective to our description of the totality of God's beauty. Wesleyans happen to look at that beauty through the jeweler's lens of holiness.

Within Protestant churches, differences among the doctrines of sanctification have been highlighted quite frequently. As is usual in such family feuds, however, the arguments are fueled by nuanced differences along a very lengthy trajectory of agreement. But some differences set our non-Wesleyan Protestant friends a bit apart from us.

*The optimism of grace versus the pessimism of sin.* The main area of contention with other Protestant views of sanctification usually is whether the grace of God is seen optimistically, with all the possibilities of human wholeness that offers, or whether human depravity makes us incapable of being holy this side of heaven. When theology is designated as "Reformed," it generally is associated with the systematic treatment of the Reformation doctrines by John Calvin and his followers. At the heart of this Reformed theology is the Lutheran preparation for worship, reminding the congregation to confess their sinfulness through "thought, word, and deed." For Luther and most of the classical Reformed tradition, the Christian life is always lived in the tension of being at the same time sinner and saint. When Wesleyans argue for the full extent of salvation, we usually argue that it must, in some way, cure our most basic problem, sin itself.

*Becoming holy versus being called holy.* A second difference is how God's grace actually changes our being. Reformed language distinguishing "imputed righteousness" (that one is called righteous) from "imparted righteousness" (that one actually *is* righteous) emphasizes that the believer is holy only by borrowing the work of Christ's cross for one's own. The believer's work of the new creation is seen as always marred, always sinful. Wesleyans, however, say, if God calls us holy, then we really must be made holy. Holy people are then capable of holy works, yet always with the power given by God's Holy Spirit.

*Spiritual vitality versus doctrinal rigidity.* The third difference really is methodological. The intellectual worldview that gave rise to the Reformation also elevated the role of the individual subject, standing alone before God, as a "priesthood of [individual] believers." It is no wonder Protestantism has fractured into its many differing sects, all claiming to have captured the spirit of authentic and biblical Christianity. Some Reformed advocates argue that their five-point Calvinism is the only true interpretation of sixteenth-century Protestantism. Even if that were the case, we no longer live in the sixteenth century. Such rigid doctrinal formulation must give way to the new intellectual context for being Christian. That context includes the diversity of human expression, freedom, and experience. The Wesleyan revivals could be seen as a "reforming of the Reformation," an attempt to offer Christianity a method that gets back to the primitive Christian concern for spiritual vitality over dogmatic pronouncements.

Despite this corrective to the dangers of a "cheap grace" Protestantism, Wesleyans always will have much to learn from dialogue with Reformed theology. A heavy dose of grace always is a healthy antidote for the burdens of legalism often associated with some perfectionist brands of holiness. When the fear of backsliding dampens the Christian's joy, the preaching of Luther again reminds us to rest and trust in Christ alone for our eternal salvation.

## HOLINESS IN ROMAN CATHOLICISM

Most Protestants have learned about Roman Catholicism by way of the prejudices created by the sixteenth-century Protestant reformers, and the political and cultural shifts of the subsequent religious upheavals in Europe. These biases often juxtaposed the corruption of medieval "popery" against the concept of "holiness" found in the list of saints and martyrs of the Roman Church. Undoubtedly, John

Wesley had many of these same prejudices against the institutional apparatus of Roman Catholicism, but he also had learned to separate the wheat from the tares as he read broadly in that august spiritual tradition.

In fact, the Roman Catholic history of the saints has had more to do with the Church as holy (*communio sanctorum*) than with the holiness of individuals, as individuals. As many of the salutations of the New Testament epistles begin by addressing the "holy and elect," so all share in the holiness of the Church by way of Christ's holiness. Still, Roman Catholicism would argue there are differences in the way people participate in that sacred community, marking off those whose exemplary lives of selfless faith spur others on to greater degrees of holiness.

The saints, martyrs, and confessors of the early persecutions gave rise to a heroic and noble form of sainthood that set such examples apart. The martyrs who spilled their blood as a witness to the shed blood of Jesus Christ were replaced, when Christianity became the established faith of Rome, with the ascetics and hermits who experienced a more self-inflicted martyrdom, the death of self. With the advent of this new form of spiritual hero, a tension also arose between holiness as a flight from the world and holiness as a transformation or sanctification of the world. Roman Catholicism today is struggling to express the holy life in a manner appropriate for contemporary Christians.

Describing the function of the saints, Karl Rahner, perhaps the twentieth century's greatest Catholic theologian, wrote,

> They are the initiators and the creative models of the holiness which happens to be right for, and is the task of, their particular age. They create a new style; they prove that a certain form of life and activity is a really genuine possibility; they

> show experimentally that one can be a Christian even in "this" way; they make such a type of person believable as a Christian type.[2]

Therefore, the saints are those who, in some way, embody the challenge of faith in their time and place. In doing so, they open a path that others might follow.

Catholics have tended to place under the rubric of "moral theology" what Wesleyans have emphasized in the doctrine of sanctification. The process of character and conscience formation is an important part of the Catholic path to holiness. The ethical life of the individual Christian is shaped while living in the church community by her catechisms (teaching), liturgy (worship), and life (holy service). Often evangelical criticisms of the Catholic Church's teachings on how one becomes a Christian are aimed at this process form of discipleship. The catechetical model of conversion offers little opportunity or encouragement for religious "crisis" experiences or spontaneous response in worship, but it does take seriously Wesley's idea that there is no real holiness without social holiness. We are shaped by the holy character of the community where we live and worship.

In the modern Catholic Church, the charismatic movement has aided in bringing about a Wesleyan-like revival among the laity. In March, 1992, Pope John Paul II spoke to those Catholics experiencing this newfound life in the Spirit:

> At this moment in the Church's history, the Charismatic Renewal can play a significant role in promoting the much-needed defense of Christian life in societies where secularism and materialism have weakened many people's ability to respond to the Spirit and to discern God's loving

> call. Your contribution to the re-evangelization of society will be made in the first place by personal witness to the indwelling Spirit and by showing forth his presence through works of holiness and solidarity.[3]

One of the possible benefits of a Wesleyan-Catholic dialogue on holiness could be, for Catholics, a better understanding of the actual usefulness of holiness for the everyday Christian. At the same time, the Catholic history of reflection on the moral authority of the cruciform conscience could prove to be a wealth of insight and help for holiness thought and practice. The Roman Catholic Church understands, as did Wesley, the doctrine of sin and the nature of the human condition more along a continuum than at a single point. Sins that are not necessarily descriptive of a Christian's heart (mistakes or ignorance) are distinguishable from those that lead to apostasy and death. As Wesley before us, Wesleyans today have a great deal to learn from the Roman Catholic spiritual traditions.

## HOLINESS IN ORTHODOX CHRISTIANITY

One of John Wesley's sources for spiritual insight was the Eastern fathers and the Hellenic Orthodox tradition.[4] One need only read ancient church authors such as Chrysostom or a desert father such as Ephraim Syrus to find similar strains of spirituality resonating with the Wesleyan emphasis on Christian perfection. When North American Christians have the opportunity to experience worship in the Eastern Orthodox Church, with its incense and iconography, they often find it strange and exotic. Westerners forget that Christianity, in its most primitive form, was an Eastern religion.

In the Orthodox Church, each baptized person is confirmed or chrismated, anointed, sealed with the gifts of the Holy Spirit, in order to share in the nature of God (2 Pet. 1:4), to participate in the holiness of God (Heb. 12:10). It is in this sense of participation in divine holiness that Paul calls the members of the community "saints." Coincidently, John Wesley read the 2 Peter text, often quoted by Orthodox theologians, on May 24, 1738, the day of his heart being "strangely warmed" at the meeting in Aldersgate Street, London. In the *Divine Liturgy* of St. John Chrysostom, still used in the Orthodox Church, occurs this refrain:

> Let our mouths be filled with Your praise, Lord, that we may sing of Your glory. You have made us worthy to partake of Your holy mysteries. Keep us in Your holiness, that all the day long we may meditate upon Your righteousness. Alleluia. Alleluia. Alleluia.

What distinguishes the Orthodox position is its ascetic, spiritual, and liturgical quest for holiness. God is holy, manifesting from his very being qualities such as goodness, justice, righteousness, beauty, and love. Orthodox theology describes the work of the indwelling Holy Spirit, whom one receives at baptism and through the sacramental life of the church, as making the divine attributes actually our own. In fact, all the Orthodox Church's activities are devoted to expressing these mysteries, through which Christians may participate in the very holiness of God. These attributes are forms of power; they radiate from God as "divine energies" communicated by the Spirit to lead each of us along the pathway of holiness that comes to its fulfillment in the kingdom of God. Ultimately, this ends with a true and eternal participation in God's very life (referred to by the Orthodox tradition as *theosis*, or "deification"). Certainly, Wesleyans would have more individualistic understandings of this participation, but much can be learned from the role of the church and her processes for "making saints" in the Orthodox Church.

St. Symeon the New Theologian, a great mystic of the Orthodox East, expressed this very well:

> I am filled with his love and I am being filled with divine joy and sweetness. I become a communicant of light and glory: my face shines like that of my beloved and all my members become radiant. Then I become more beautiful than the beautiful, richer than the rich; I become stronger than all the strong, greater than emperors and much more honorable than anything ever seen, not only of the earth and what is on earth, but also heaven and everything that is in heaven.[5]

What this mystical experience of *theosis* does for the individual, the Orthodox also claim for the *cosmos*, the world. The ultimate restoration to the pre-fallen state of the creation under God is the final healing to Shalom and wholeness.

With the collapse of the Soviet Union, and the new context for exchange and cooperation with Eastern Christians, Western Christianity can benefit by learning from the rich, ancient traditions of Orthodox worship and practice.

The Orthodox Christian knows the ultimate end of all things is found only in God. Experiencing inwardly the real, authentic God, we are reminded of the deathbed words attributed to John Wesley: "The best of all is, God is with us!" It is not enough to experience salvation, or even to obtain some static state of holiness, if it misses the "best" part—a restored and actively lived relationship with God.

## HOLINESS IN THE WORLD OUTSIDE THE CHURCH

As Dietrich Bonhoeffer pointed out half a century ago, Christians need to learn from examples—not just the saints of long ago, but examples from all quadrants of the world.[6] Quite often this means seeing God at work in people different than ourselves both theologically and culturally. For Bonhoeffer, Mahatma Gandhi was such a person of holiness.

The idea that all people are predisposed toward the Spirit—not a uniquely Wesleyan view, but one Wesley methodologically reflected upon—allows for saintly examples to be applauded and followed wherever they are found. In today's world, we often are embarrassed to find the Church in short supply of saints, while benevolence and charity are lived out even in the secular marketplace. The holiness of the Triune God is involved everywhere in the world, even as sin and evil permeate the brokenness of all things.

One of John Wesley's well-known sermons on this topic is the "Catholic Spirit." His text for that famous homily is 2 Kings 10:15 (NRSV): "[Jehu said,] 'Is your heart as true to mine as mine is to yours?' Jehonadab answered, 'It is.' Jehu said, 'If it is, give me your hand.'" In this sermon, Wesley gives a detailed description of what it means for one's heart to be right. It is "right" if it is right with God, if it believes in the Lord Jesus Christ, if it is "filled with the energy of love," if it is doing the will of God, if it serves the Lord with reverence, if it is right toward one's neighbor, and if it shows love by what it does.

Interestingly, this "catholic spirit" is to be shown to those outside the faith, as well as to those within the fellowship of Christians. Regarding those outside the faith, Wesley said that the person with a catholic spirit "embraces with strong and cordial affection neighbors and strangers, friends and enemies. This is catholic or universal love. And he that has this is of a catholic spirit. For love alone gives the title to this character: catholic love is a catholic spirit."[7]

After defining "catholic spirit" in this very inclusive way, Wesley then dealt with it in relation to fellow believers. He referred to love for "all, of whatever opinion or worship or congregation, who believe in the Lord Jesus Christ, who love God and man, who, rejoicing to please and fearing to offend God, are careful to abstain from evil and zealous of good works." Continuing, Wesley says that the one who is of a truly catholic spirit,

> having an unspeakable tenderness for their persons and longing for their welfare, does not cease to commend them to God in prayer as well as to plead their cause before men; who speaks comfortably to them and labors by all his words to strengthen their hands in God. He assists them to the uttermost of his power in all things, spiritual and temporal. He is ready "to spend and be spent for them" [compare 2 Cor. 12:15], yea, "to lay down his life for' their sake" [John 15:13].[8]

For his time, Wesley had a great deal of openness toward people of differing worldviews or church affiliations, and he sought to discover larger levels of cooperation in the Christian life and within the human family at large. We need today to follow Wesley's excellent example, for never has there been a better time for Wesleyan-Holiness Christians to enter into dialogue with the wider Christian communion, and beyond. For one thing, such an inspired conversation will offer to the beleaguered contemporary church both a doctrinal content and a method for expressing the value of being a Christian in today's world. Just as important, we too will have an opportunity to learn from representatives of diverse faiths, not necessarily to reconcile their adherents into full, organic unity with one another, but simply to promote better relations. Mutual respect and cooperation even among Christian denominations and traditions will start when we acknowledge God's sanctifying activity at work in all creation.

Missiologists are alerting us to the ethnocentric features of Western theology. Timothy Tennent, in *Theology in the Context of*

*World Christianity*, said, "Many of the hottest and most passionate cultural and theological debates currently going on . . . seem trite from the perspective of Asian or African Christianity. We must learn to think bigger, listen more, and look at the church from a wider vista."[9] In the context of our discussion of holiness, Tennent cautioned us to be careful not to allow our formulations about this doctrine to be truncated by its location in the Anglo-American context. He went on to say,

> On the one hand I want to clearly affirm the magnificent universal truths of the gospel that are true for all people, of all cultures, throughout all time. On the other hand, I also affirm that there is much we can learn from the particular insights of the emerging global church. I also believe there is much that we can offer the newer churches outside the West because of our background and years of sustained theological reflection. Likewise, they can help to fill in the gaps in our own theological reflection, especially by exposing areas where our reflection has been biased and resistant to the actual teaching of Scripture.[10]

## HOLINESS IS LARGER THAN WE KNEW

Faith is something we do, not something we merely know. The connection between true orthodoxy and orthopraxy, between what we believe and what we do, always will be evidenced by the fruit of the Spirit. In the eighteenth century, Wesley was onto something most people today still are trying to grasp. He was more concerned with being holy toward God than with establishing a paradigm that made sense for all cultures and all ages. We may never come up with a formula that completely describes the common experience of holiness, because our understanding of God is never perfect. But by listening to the many voices in the Christian tradition of holy practice we can get closer to a fuller understanding of this important doctrine.

May the Church so develop her teachings on holiness, not merely to be right, but that her people actually embrace holiness!

## ACTION/REFLECTION SUGGESTIONS

**1.** Visit with ministers or practitioners outside your own faith background. Ask general questions of each other, such as, "What would a holy person look like in your church?" and "What is the theological basis for grace?" Learn to listen, and share insights from your own background with humility and care.

**2.** In public prayer, as well as in your personal prayer life, support the Church in our common quest for holiness in the world. When praying for mission outreach, remember to pray for all the churches and persons serving Christ around the globe.

**3.** Consider how holiness can be expressed and taught that will lead to socially transforming church activities. What steps will you take to make this transition a reality in your congregation?

## NOTES

1. Brian McLaren, *A Generous Orthodoxy* (Grand Rapids, Mich.: Zondervan, 2004), 136. This popular, important book has this provocative subtitle: *Why I Am a Missional, Evangelical, Post/Protestant, Liberal/Conservative, Mystical/Poetic, Biblical, Charismatic/Contemplative, Fundamentalist/Calvinist, Anabaptist/Anglican, Methodist, Catholic, Green, Incarnational, Depressed-yet-Hopeful, Emergent, Unfinished CHRISTIAN.*

2. Karl Rahner, "The Church of the Saints," in Karl-H. and Boniface Kruger (trans.), *Theological Investigations*, vol. 3 (Baltimore: Helicon, 1967), 100.

3. Address of Pope John Paul II to the council of the International Catholic Charismatic Renewal Office (ICCRO), March 14, 1992. http://www.vatican.va/holy_father/john_paul_ii/speeches/1992/march/documents/hf_jp-ii_spe_19920314_charismatic-renewal_en.html. He later declared, at the start of the twenty-first century, that the third millennium would be characterized by an emphasis on the Holy Spirit.

4. See Randy L. Maddox, "John Wesley and Eastern Orthodoxy: Influences, Convergences, and Differences," *Asbury Theological Journal* 45 no. 2 (1990): 29–53, for a very helpful comparison of Orthodox ideas with those of Wesley.

5. Quoted in Nicolas Berdyaev, "Salvation and Creativity: Two Understandings of Christianity," in Matthew Fox, ed., *Western Spirituality: Historical Roots, Ecumenical Routes* (Notre Dame, Ind: Fides/Claretian, 1979), 126.

6. Dietrich Bonhoeffer, *Letters and Papers from Prison* (New York: SCM, 1971), 211.

7. See Albert C. Outler, ed. *John Wesley* (New York: Oxford University Press, 1964), 91–104.

8. Ibid., 103.

9. Timothy C. Tennent, *Theology in the Context of World Christianity* (Grand Rapids, Mich.: Zondervan, 2007), xviii.

10. Ibid., 13.

# PREACHING HOLINESS TODAY

*J. Michael Walters*

*Ascribe to the* L*ORD* *the glory due his name;*
*worship the* L*ORD* *in the splendor of his holiness.*

—Psalm 29:2

*The land was dotted with small trees called* palo santo—
*"holy stick" in English. . . . They had leaves only in the wet season, . . . Kerry explained. Neo commented on the irony of the name. "Holy sticks should be vibrant and green and fruitful not bare and gray. Holiness is beautiful and vigorous, not ugly and barren."*

—Brian McClaren, *The Story We Find Ourselves In*

In a *Christianity Today* article titled "Holy to the Core," author Joel Scandrett suggested that conventional evangelical wisdom these days holds that talking about holiness to people you're trying to win to Christ is dangerously stupid.

Let the irony of that sink in. When it comes to proclaiming Jesus, "contemporary" Christian "experts" are promoting a "what's holiness got to do with it?" attitude and approach.

Of course, as Scandrett pointed out, "For many American evangelicals, 'holiness' conjures up musty images of revival meetings, gospel trios, and old-time religion—along with stern prohibitions against drinking, dancing and playing cards."[1] To those who cling to this caricature, holiness is anything but beautiful, so "Let's keep Jesus and holiness in separate rooms," they advise not so subtly, "preferably with the holiness room locked from the outside!"

## HOLINESS IS THE IMPERATIVE

Those of us who are serious about preaching holiness in the twenty-first century certainly must recognize the need for careful, and perhaps extensive, damage control, lest the message of biblical holiness be rejected out of hand, due to the harsh and painful past experiences of some of our hearers. But all the extremes, all the aberrations that can be cited notwithstanding, *whether* one will preach holiness is not an open question for anyone serious about the Bible—nor for anyone serious about Jesus.

The pastoral question here, I think, is, What is it going to take for people to believe holiness is "beautiful and vigorous, not ugly and barren"? *This* is the challenge of preaching holiness in this day.

Clearly, we must preach this message; it is part and parcel of the good news! That is the positive reason, and it is paramount. But the negative reason is important to grasp, also.

If current conditions tell us anything, they demonstrate the absolute and pressing imperative of bringing professing Christians to a deeper knowledge of God. The cold reality is that unless we find a way to deepen the spiritual life of the average North American church member, this culture will swallow most of them whole.

The last third of the twentieth century, which seemed so "successful" in terms of evangelism, failed to produce the legions of mature disciples that such "success" should have brought forth. The spiritual nurseries of our churches have been full to overflowing, but those moving on to maturity have proven to be an uncomfortably small percentage of the "harvest." Dallas Willard framed the issue starkly:

> It is, I gently suggest, a serious error to make "outreach" a *primary* goal of the local congregation, and especially so when those who are already "with us" have not become clear-headed and devoted apprentices of Jesus, and are not, for the most part, solidly progressing along the path. Outreach is one essential task of Christ's people, and among them there will always be those especially gifted for evangelism. But the most successful work of outreach would be the work of *inreach* that turns people, wherever they are, into lights in the darkened world.[2]

Being an apprentice or disciple of Jesus is, in fact, the very heart of the Christian life, and upon closer inspection it appears Jesus isn't nearly as gun shy about holiness as are many of his contemporary followers. Biblically, theologically, or even pragmatically, the question isn't whether we should preach holiness; the question is, "How?" What's it going to take to get modern people to believe holiness is beautiful? Let alone practical and attainable?

As mentioned previously, we will need to do sometimes-extensive repair work to overcome built-in prejudices or painful memories that some associate with the holiness message. Further, it may be useful to dispel the commonly held associations between holiness and separatism with "real life." The church of Jesus Christ cannot come off as culture despisers. That may have been part of our game plan in the old holiness playbook, but it has to go. We will not win the world if we hate its cultures, including our own.

I can think of no better way to demonstrate the true concern and unstinting involvement of holiness with its surrounding environment than to look at the life of Wesley himself, and at the early Wesleyan Methodists in this country. These were people whose commitment to holiness was unquestioned, and that commitment played itself out in a wholehearted investment into the world around them. There is no sound reason for associating true biblical holiness with the kind of "hide behind the walls of the fortress" mentality that has too often been our stance. Enabling people to recognize how holiness has been caricatured and misapplied, just like many other elements within our faith, can break down the defensiveness of modern listeners.

It's not enough, however, simply to demythologize our holiness past. Let me suggest one broad principle that ought to underlie our preaching of this doctrine, and then some thematic entry points in urging our twenty-first-century listeners "on to perfection."

## STICK WITH THE BIG PICTURE

By choosing the big-picture approach to preaching about holiness, I mean primarily two things: first, to grasp clearly that holiness is not a "Wesleyan" thing; and, second, to preach holiness as foundational to the wholeness of human life.

Growing up, I labored under the false supposition that we were a holiness church because other churches didn't believe in it. Not so. As other essays in this book amply demonstrate, holiness is not reserved for advanced or mature Christians; neither is it only for Wesleyans. The call to a holy life stands at the beginning and center of God's call on our lives. Moreover, it is a fundamental mistake to assume this truth has been missed or ignored by other faith communities. As an example, consider these words:

> The work of Jesus in the world is twofold. It is a work accomplished *for us*, destined to effect *reconciliation* between God and man; it is a work accomplished *in us*, with the object of effecting our *sanctification*. By the one a right *relation* is established between God and us; by the other, the *fruit* of the reestablished order is secured. By the former, the condemned

> sinner is received into the state of grace; by the latter the pardoned sinner is associated with the life of God. . . . How many express themselves as if, when forgiveness with the peace which it procures has been once obtained, all is finished and the work of salvation is complete! They seem to have no suspicion that salvation consists in the health of the soul, and that the health of the soul consists in holiness. Forgiveness is not the reestablishment of health; it is the crisis of convalescence. If God thinks fit to declare the sinner righteous, it is in order that he may by that means restore him to holiness.[3]

These words are quoted from the *Systematic Theology* of Augustus H. Strong, one of the preeminent Baptist theologians of modern times. This isn't *our* message; it's the Bible's message. We must not preach holiness solely as a Wesleyan idea. It's a biblical idea, and the better job we do of demonstrating that to our people, the more receptive they will be.

Further, we want to take care to avoid what I call the "mixed-messages" approach. This is where personal holiness is championed over social holiness, or vice versa. There is no conflict here. It's *wholiness.* Life is systemic, connected. The gospel is all encompassing. JohnWesley figured out that if the Holy Spirit dwelt in the hearts of men and women, God could not only transform individuals but society, as well. And transform it, he did. We have heard the stories of Wesleyans throwing themselves into the abolition of slavery, the establishment of the rights of women, access to public education, the reform of prisons and the redemption of prisoners—into active concern for any aspect of human experience that affects the well-being of people. That kind of commitment to society is part and parcel of authentic Wesleyan spirituality, regardless of how little we may see it manifested today. Holiness is God's plan for the entire world, not just for human hearts.

The emphasis upon wholeness necessarily moves us out of the confines of personal spirituality into the struggles for justice and righteousness in our culture. The generation with which we work is hungry to see the relevance of the gospel to real life. Holiness, rightly proclaimed, demonstrates such. For example, having read a good deal of Wesley's writings, it's hard for me to imagine him being silent today on the subject of creation care. Does not holiness have a creational, or ecological, dimension to it? This is God's world, not ours. Holy people would be the best possible stewards of creation.

Wesleyan pastors ought to speak to the broader implications of what it means to be wholly consecrated to God and to his plan for his world. Holiness, it turns out, is as wide as life. It is about wholeness for the human condition, and that means good news for all creation, as well. Preaching holiness as a narrow, binding experience robs it of its power to transform.

Mildred Bangs Wynkoop, one of the finest interpreters of holiness doctrine in our tradition, has pointed out that, in all the aberrations regarding perfection in the experience of the Church in history, a compartmentalization of life is a characteristic of the faulty view. Wesley's position was that the more seriously perfection is held, the more compartmentalization is broken up and the life unified and strengthened. Holiness of heart doesn't remain in the heart; it spreads to all other areas of life. The very nature of holiness is to interpenetrate that which is around it. We must proclaim a "whole" gospel to the whole world. "There is a cross in the Christian life, but the cross is not an end of the self. It is an end of the sin that shackles the self and blocks the way to goodness. The cross is always at the *beginning of life*. The whole of real life lies beyond it."[4]

## FIVE TALKING POINTS FOR PREACHING HOLINESS

What follows are simply thematic entry points I would consider using to preach holiness. Clearly, this is not an exhaustive list, and other preachers well may have their own preferred gateways into this vital message. But let me suggest the following five.

*1. It's about Jesus*

First, pure and simple, it's about Jesus. As Mildred Wynkoop put it in her timeless essay from 1969, "Preaching holiness is preaching Christ."[5] Jesus was a holy man. He personifies what holiness is. As we look at him closely, we see that he is, in fact, "wholeness incarnate." Scandrett observed, "Many American Christians see Jesus as little more than a means of augmenting their sense of self, either as a source of 'health and prosperity' or of emotional 'well-being.'"[6] This view of Jesus *cannot* be supported by the texts of the Gospels, and pastors would do well to teach their people the real Jesus of Scripture.

Interestingly, Jesus didn't *say* much about holiness. He simply lived a holy life in front of his contemporaries and called them to follow him. In *Truth Is Stranger Than It Used to Be,* Richard Middleton and Brian Walsh note that the prophetic ministry of Jesus is characterized by the "almost complete absence of the popular first-century concept of holiness." They contend this is no accident. Jesus, in their view, avoided the term because of how it had been misused by the Pharisees and the scribes. Rather than using the call to holiness as an excuse to exclude others, Jesus demonstrated the inclusiveness of holiness by his relationships with the outcasts of Jewish society. In so doing, Jesus recaptured the essence of Israel's call to be a "holy nation" (Ex. 19:4–6) and, thus, to be the means by which the whole world would be blessed.[7] We should take this to heart. Rather than trying to argue doctrinal nuances with people who have little patience with theology, we should show them Jesus, continually. Jesus is the single best advertisement for the holy life.

2. *It's about Being like Jesus*

Call it discipleship; call it Christlikeness; call it making Jesus Lord of our lives; call it consecration; call it whatever, but the end, the goal (Greek, *telos*), is the same: to be like Jesus. A disciple is like his or her master. One can't go very far down the road of authentic discipleship without bringing in the call to holiness. Not that we haven't tried! The soft-sided approaches to evangelism of the past few decades, emphasizing only the need to "trust Jesus," have not proven effective routes toward becoming apprentices of Jesus. To quote Dallas Willard again:

> A fundamental mistake of the conservative side of the American church today, and much of the Western church, is that it takes as its *basic* goal to get as many people as possible ready to die and go to heaven. It aims to get people into heaven rather than to get heaven into people. This of course requires that these people, who are going to be "in," must be *right* on what is basic. You can't really quarrel with that. But it turns out that to be right on "what is basic" is to be *right* in terms of the particular church vessel or tradition in question, not in terms of Christlikeness.[8]

I contend that the solution to this is to preach the necessity of discipleship defined as actually obeying "all that [Jesus] commanded" (Matt. 28:20 NASB). If we can bring people to this point in their lives, holiness will be the end product. Preach discipleship, the intentional adoption of Jesus' practices and attitudes. This will require radical dependence upon the Holy Spirit, and will allow him the freedom to do what only he can do in the lives of people.

3. *It's a Relationship*

Holiness is a relationship, not a transaction. One of the enduring memories of my own heritage in the church is of hearing the testimonies of people who claimed to have received "the blessing" in much the same way we might speak of having received a Christmas gift. It was offered, we received it, and that was that. This legal, or "forensic," understanding of holiness is actually far afield from the Scriptures. The Hebrew root for "holy" (*qadash*) connotes "belonging to God"; it's a relational term. Holiness describes an intimate relationship with God; it is not simply a transaction made at some point in time. By virtue of our relationship with Jesus Christ, we participate in the life of God. Rather than going through life obeying rules, we deal with far more fundamental questions, such as, "Whose are we? To whom do we give our first love and loyalty?"[9] These are relational questions.

One important implication of this, I think, is that preachers need to emphasize the "journey" of holiness, rather than simply the "crisis." Mildred Wynkoop spoke of the danger of stressing "methodology" (how it's done) to the extent that the "moral, personal, and life relevance [of holiness] is almost totally obscured."[10] I don't mean we can't talk about the "crises" that are part of any spiritual journey; no, the crisis is real. Willard put it well:

> Sanctification in this life will always be a matter of degree, to be sure, but there is a point in genuine spiritual growth before which the term "sanctification" simply does not apply—just as "hot" when applied to a cup of coffee is a matter of degree, but there is a point before which it is not hot, even if in the process of being heated.[11]

So, holiness must be presented as a continuous process rather than a "once and done" transaction; it continues for the rest of life. Wesley himself couldn't have been more clear on this point:

> Walk in all the good works whereunto ye are created in Christ Jesus. And, "leaving the principles of the doctrine of Christ and not laying again the foundation of repentance from dead works, and of faith toward God," go on to perfection. Yea, and when ye have attained a measure of perfect love, when God has circumcised your hearts, and enabled you to love him with all your heart and with all your soul, *think not of resting there. That is impossible. You cannot stand still; you must either rise or fall; rise higher or fall lower.* Therefore the voice of God to the Children of Israel, to the children of God, is "Go forward." "Forgetting the things that are behind and reaching forward unto those things that are before, press on to the mark, for the prize of your high calling of God in Christ Jesus."[12]

We must remind our people that repentance is, according to Wesley, merely the porch of salvation. God wants to inhabit the entire house, and that entails the surrender of the will to allow him entry. Precisely because the human will is multilayered or, at least, extremely complicated, Wesleyan spirituality has maintained that the question of the will is not generally settled in one moment of crisis. Preaching this point enables our people to relax and allow God to work in them on the basis of their relationship with him, rather than fretting over whether or not "the work was really done." As Wynkoop put it, "Holiness has no ceiling. It's as big as the future, and more challenging than the deepest capacity any person can fully explore."[13]

One would expect nothing else of a relationship between a holy God and persons created in God's own image. Preaching intimacy in our experience with God is a direct entry way onto the highway called holiness.

*4. It's Personal, but not Individual*

Wesley's famous maxim about "holy solitaries" being as impossible as "holy adulterers" is more than just a good line—it's the truth. The call to holiness is a call to a corporate life in the church that transcends the individualism so rampant in American culture. Scandrett said it this way:

> The church is God's crucible and matrix for forming holy lives in many ways. . . . From the beginning, God has intended that his covenant people be the means by which all the nations of the world are blessed. Far from leading to self-righteous, world-abnegating sectarianism, true biblical holiness leads us to participate in the ministry of reconciliation that God has given to his people.[14]

The *Church* is called to holiness. Not to emphasize the corporate dimensions of holiness is to set people up for failure. Wesley lamented that "converts without nurture are like stillborn babies." Regarding the vulnerability of newborn converts, he wrote in his journal,

> I was more convinced than ever that the preaching like an Apostle, without joining together those that are awakened and training them up in the ways of God, is only begetting children for the murderer.[15]

It was out of this deep conviction regarding the nurture of believers that the famous "class meetings" became a staple of Wesleyan spiritual formation. Weekly meetings of Christians aimed at fostering confession, accountability, encouragement, and the constant monitoring, *in community*, of one's relationship with God were standard operating procedures. Preaching holiness in the twenty-first century entails preaching biblical ecclesiology, as well as a counterbalance to the destructive individualism that keeps people locked into their delusions of autonomy. A holy person is produced by a holy people. A healthy, vital church is indispensable to that goal.

*5. It's all about Love*

In 1 Timothy 1, Paul urged the young pastor Timothy to command certain men not to teach false doctrine and to stop devoting themselves to matters that only lead to controversy in the church. In verse 5, he made this interesting comment: "The goal of this command is love, which comes from a pure heart and a good conscience and a sincere faith."

"Love is the atmosphere of holiness, and love is the expenditure of the self. In the best sense of the word, holiness cannot happen in a moment. It may begin in a moment, but as love cannot mature without expression, so holiness, which is love, cannot exist apart from the life expression of it."[16] This statement from Mildred Wynkoop perfectly connects the all-important relational element of the holy life with its only legitimate end: love. If we can stick to talking to our people about a love relationship with our holy God, it's hard to imagine they would either be confused by the concept or repelled by its aims. At the end of the day, and at the end of the sermon, it's all about love. We are called to be in a vital, intimate love relationship with our God.

Speaking of love, on Friday, June 7, 1974, I walked into Estes Chapel on the campus of Asbury Theological Seminary to get myself married. About an hour after it started, that ceremony ended and I walked out a married man. Legally, in the eyes of God, the state of

Kentucky, and a couple hundred witnesses, I was married. In terms of my *legal* status, I was as married then as I ever will be.

At that point, I suppose I could have looked at my new bride, wished her well, hopped into the car with my buddies, and headed off to go fishing for a few weeks. I mean, I *am* married, after all. Legally, I'm just as married at the lake as anywhere else. Regardless of whether I actually *see* my wife or spend any time with her, legally and technically I'm married.

Of course, if I had done that, you would be perfectly justified in judging me insane. I would have completely missed the point of getting married. I can hear you shouting inside your head now, "It's a *relationship*, stupid!"

Sadly, though, we have churches filled with people whose "legal" status with God seems clear, at least according to them. But their love for God, their relationship with God, leaves much to be desired. We have a message from our holy God urging us to come home to him, effectively to "marry" ourselves to him, and through the abiding presence of the Holy Spirit, to learn the joys of eternal friendship and communion. There is no greater privilege afforded to a preacher than to officiate at that ceremony. Like weddings, holiness is beautiful. Preach it that way.

## ACTION/REFLECTION SUGGESTIONS

**1.** Study the following passages carefully and prayerfully to see how they can help you to preach, teach, and encourage your people to seek the holy life: Psalm 40; Isaiah 58; Matthew 5—7; Colossians 3; 1 Thessalonians 5:23–24; James 4:1–10; 2 Peter 1.

**2.** Make it a regular habit to think about your local church situation, your neighborhood, your town, your region, and our world through the lens of this question: What would it mean to be holy people in each of these contexts?

**3.** Arrange a series of conversations with people in your church, either individually or in small groups. Ask them first to share their immediate reactions to words such as *holiness*, *sanctification*, *total surrender*, the *lordship of Christ*. Then ask them about Jesus, about his life and attitudes, and continue (or resume at another time) the dialogue long enough to make sure they see the connection between Jesus and holiness.

## NOTES

1. Joel Scandrett, "Holy to the Core," *Christianity Today* (May 2007), 39.
2. Dallas Willard, *Renovation of the Heart* (Colorado Springs: NavPress, 2002), 244.
3. Augustus H. Strong, cited in Willard, *Renovation*, 224.
4. Mildred Bangs Wynkoop, "A Wesleyan View on Preaching Holiness," *Wesleyan Theological Journal* (Spring 1969), 20.
5. Ibid., 19.
6. Scandrett, "Holy," 40.
7. J. Richard Middleton and Brian J. Walsh, *Truth Is Stranger Than It Used to Be* (Downers Grove, Ill.: InterVarsity, 1995), 103.
8. Willard, *Renovation*, 238–239.
9. Scandrett, "Holy," 39.
10. Wynkoop, "A Wesleyan View," 16.
11. Willard, *Renovation*, 226.
12. John Wesley, *Works*, vol. VII (Grand Rapids, Mich.: Baker, 1996), 202.
13. Wynkoop, "A Wesleyan View, 18.
14. Scandrett, "Holy," 40.
15. John Wesley, *Works*, vol. III, 144.
16. Wynkoop, "A Wesleyan View," 20.

8

# EXPERIENCING THE HOLY LIFE

*Keith Drury*

*May God himself, the God of peace, sanctify you through and through. May your whole spirit, soul and body be kept blameless at the coming of our Lord Jesus Christ. The one who calls you is faithful and he will do it.*

—1 Thessalonians 5:23–24

*God loves you just the way you are, but he refuses to leave you that way.*

—Max Lucado

Jason had been raised in a holiness church, but he didn't know it. He was an active leader in his youth group and testified to a call into the ministry at age seventeen. As a college sophomore he encountered his first class in theology. There a professor explained the doctrine of entire sanctification, but Jason was sure he was being taught false doctrine. He went to his mentor, complaining, "He's teaching stuff Wesleyans don't believe." His mentor asked him to explain. What followed was a lucid description of entire sanctification about the way John Wesley would have done it. Jason's mentor smiled and said, "Give it some time and see how this teaching fits with your denomination's stance." Jason left the appointment only partially satisfied. The mentor turned to his computer screen chuckling to himself.

The notion of entire sanctification is in a bear market, though emphasis on progressive sanctification is having a heyday. Young people raised in churches that claim to believe in the doctrine sometimes think it is heresy when they hear it. "I've never heard that idea before," they say. Or, "If this doctrine is true, how come we never heard it before?"

This doctrine is not new; it is rooted in Scripture and the teachings of the early church fathers. But it is more than a theory for biblical and historical study; it can be a real daily experience for God's followers. *Believing* in holiness does not make a holy people, but *receiving* this work of grace changes our walk with God and our work with others. This chapter is about the ways we can experience holiness in our daily life—how believers can change into the people God intended us to be.

## BECOMING ALL WE WERE MEANT TO BE

*Holiness is Christlikeness.* Holiness is living a Christlike life in word, thought, and deed. Thus, holiness often is seen as "perfect love"—a complete love for God and others that fulfills the two great commandments: loving God with all our heart, mind, soul, and strength, and loving others as ourselves. It sounds like an impossible dream to those who have been taught "Nobody's perfect." Yet God in his Word calls us to be perfect (in the sense of "complete"), so how do we receive holiness, or become holy?

*We become holy through sanctification.* Sanctification is everything God does in us to make us more like Christ.

*Some things happen outside us when we submit to Christ.* For instance, we are *adopted* into the family of God and we are *justified*, making us not guilty. Adoption and justification do not happen inside us, but are legal transactions that occur in the courts of heaven. Sanctification happens inside us—bringing change in who we are.

## PREVENIENT GRACE

*Sanctification starts when we are saved, or maybe even before.* When did you start changing inside? For some, the first change happens the moment they believe, but many others begin changing even before they are saved. God's grace reaches out to us while we are yet sinners, and enlivens our hearts so we *want* to be saved. In our fallen state, we humans are dead in our trespasses and sins, too darkened even to reach out to God without God's help.

This help is called *prevenient grace*—the grace of God that goes before justification. This grace enables us to believe, enables us to *want* to be saved. The hunger for God is not something we work up on our own—this too comes from God, and by this grace we may begin to change even before we completely submit to Christ.

Not all Christians recall this *prevenient sanctification*, but many do. While technically this grace-that-precedes salvation usually is categorized under the heading of "grace," it also can be considered as the beginning of sanctification.

## INITIAL SANCTIFICATION

*The immediate change accompanying conversion is called initial sanctification.* When you were converted, God changed you, not only in position (as our Reformed brothers and sisters rightly stress) but also in fact. In position, you were (and are) "in Christ," raised to be seated in Christ at the right hand of the Father, perfect in Christ. But more than your "theoretical" position changed when you believed. You also experienced an actual change at conversion—inside you. Old things passed away. Things became new. Some of your old habits fell away the moment you believed. New desires rushed in. Your language may have changed. Your thoughts changed, and your deeds were different. This all occurred by God's grace at conversion. Conversion means change, and the change is both in position and in performance. Indeed, this is what sanctification is all about—ultimately, to bring our actual performance up to our perfect position in Christ.

*Initial sanctification occurs around the moment of conversion.* It happens in an instant or at least in a short time. It changes what we are inside, as we take a giant leap toward being like Christ. For an adult chained by habits of sin, initial sanctification can be dramatic. For "good kids" raised by Christian parents in the church, the change is less dramatic but still just as real. This is initial sanctification—God making us more like Christ, but it is only the beginning.

## PROGRESSIVE SANCTIFICATION

*Conversion does not complete the job of making us like Christ.* As we have said, sanctification is God's work of bringing our performance up to our perfect position in Christ. The work of our initial sanctification in a moment (or short period) is now followed by *progressive sanctification*—God works gradually and steadily in making us more like Christ.

How does God do this? The Holy Spirit first convicts us. By reading and studying Scripture, by hearing instructive preaching or the testimony of another—often by several means together—we become convinced that something needs changing in our lives. We may deny this prompting at first, or delay yielding for a time, but eventually (if we have been truly converted) we will surrender. Maybe it is conviction of *wrong deeds*—actions, habits, and behaviors that are out of place in the Christlike life. Or, perhaps the Spirit convicts us about *wrong words* we use, such as cutting remarks, stretching the truth, telling half-truths, or gossiping. Or, the Spirit may convict us of *wrong thoughts*—envy, sexual fantasies, or selfish motivations. Whatever the issues may be, the Spirit convinces us that even though we are saved, *this* word, thought, or deed is improper for a devoted Christ-follower. What will we do? We will confess these things and yield to God, seeking his changing power.

*Conviction comes with hope for deliverance.* This is one way we can tell the difference between the Spirit's conviction and the devil's condemnation. Like the Spirit, the Accuser also reminds us of sin; but the devil condemns us for it, producing despair, while the Spirit convinces us with hope in God's changing power. When we yield to the Spirit's conviction, we confess and seek God's changing power.

*God's changing power in progressive sanctification may come in an instant, or it may come gradually.* Have you ever been changed in a moment? Maybe you attended a retreat or heard a sermon where you fell under conviction, yielded immediately, and were changed—all in the space of an hour or less. God "delivered" you.

More often today, however, Christians tell about their gradual deliverance in one area or another. They tell about the Spirit's conviction and the gradual process of change God has brought about in their lives. It may have been over a few months or even several years, but eventually these Christians can testify about complete deliverance.

Either way—the short route or the long one—describes progressive sanctification. We do not know why God takes the longer or the shorter way with a believer, but God uses both means. Who would tell a man caught up in an adulterous affair, "Hold on and God will help you gradually wind down the frequency of your adulteries"? Even the unsaved world expects him to stop at once. While we do not accept the notion of a "recovering adulterer," we do allow such thinking for many other sins. Either way we change, whether instantaneously or gradually, when we put off sin and put on the words, thoughts, and deeds of Christlikeness, we are experiencing progressive sanctification by God's power.

*God's changing power may come through human help, or it may come "spiritually."* God sometimes works a direct miracle of deliverance in us "spiritually," during a church service, when we go forward to pray during an altar call, or even when we are somewhere alone in prayer. Other times, God works through people, such as when he delivers us through counseling, an accountability group, or a twelve-step recovery program. In either case, God still is sanctifying us progressively, though it seems more obvious to us when it is wholly "spiritual."

Physical healing is a good parallel model here. We all believe God can heal directly and miraculously. People have been healed of cancer in a moment while sitting in church. But God also heals cancer through radiation, chemotherapy, and surgery. In either case we give God credit for healing. Most of us today seek human help first, asking God to use doctors to heal us. This is similar to how we approach spiritual healing today. When a person is hooked on pornography or alcohol, we tend to steer him or her into recovery and ask God to help or (if God should act miraculously) to hasten the process.

We live in a culture of Western evangelical gradualism, where miraculous deliverance is rare or even disbelieved altogether. In such a culture it is difficult to get people to believe God *can* heal them (physically or spiritually) in an instant. Thus, God's work seems to be mostly limited to being an ally to human help. We mostly ask God to bless the doctor or counselor as he or she provides the healing. No matter. Either way, the change that comes is from God—through human help guided by God, or through miraculous deliverance provided directly from and by God. In both ways (to return to the "spiritual" issues), God is progressively sanctifying us.

*Progressive sanctification continues as we continually yield.* The Spirit can be relied on to bring "new light." When we respond and "walk in the light," we will become more like Christ. We are speaking here not only of stopping sin, but also of putting on righteousness. Certainly sin has no place in the life of a believer, but even if we have crucified every single sin listed in the Bible, we still have more growing to do. We also are instructed and encouraged to add the full virtue of Christ. Progressive sanctification is the means through which God makes us like Christ gradually. One by one, the sins in our life are mortified and put off as God delivers us. One by one, righteous words, thoughts, and deeds are expanded as we are transformed into the image of Jesus Christ.

## ENTIRE SANCTIFICATION

*Everything we have said so far is basic Christian doctrine.* All Protestant, Catholic, and Orthodox Christians accept the notions of initial and progressive sanctification. We now move beyond basic doctrine to a special teaching of some early church fathers and of John Wesley—*entire sanctification.*

We could say this idea begins with the observation that most Christians get "stuck" in their walk of progressive sanctification and quit yielding. It does not have to be that way but seems to be true of most. They overcome the worst sins, or the outer sins, then get satisfied with their state and quit growing. Maybe they have a pet sin that seems too hard to beat or to give up. Or there are righteous attitudes that just seem too hard to develop. So they give up and progress grinds to a halt.

With forward progress halted, they sometimes even fall back into old sins. Outside they may appear fine, but inside they harbor wrong thoughts and motivations. They cannot say they are "fully devoted followers of Jesus Christ." They are partially devoted—maybe even *mostly* devoted—but not fully so.

*Many Christians settle for this defeated life.* They may say, "This is all there is." They may argue, "I'm only human, and I'm stuck with being this way until I get to heaven." Many never even have heard there is any other way to live.

*In entire sanctification, God completes the work of progressive sanctification.* He does so while we are still here on earth. This teaching of John Wesley and others says we are not stuck forever being part-time devotees to God. God can finish the work he began in us. He can make us *fully* devoted followers of Jesus Christ. It is something like a second conversion, and it is not something we can work for; it, too, comes by receiving God's work of grace by faith and only when we abandon our own agenda and cast ourselves completely into God's hands in total surrender.

We seek God's complete work until we experience it. We say, "If we are commanded to love God with all our hearts, it must actually be possible to do so, so I am seeking this work of love in my heart so I can be a fully devoted follower of Jesus Christ." We knock until the door is opened. We ask until we receive. We seek until we find.

*Seeking entire sanctification is rare today*. Folk will give several years of their lives to a recovery process or to therapy, but only a few minutes seeking entire sanctification before giving up and dismissing the possibility as a vain hope. Yet God has promised to make us complete. We are not destined to be stuck as part-time God-lovers. We can be made wholly holy. If we will consecrate our all to him and reach out in faith believing he can do his work, then seek him until we find his transformation, it can come even today in our culture of evangelical gradualism. This is the optimistic hope of entire sanctification the early church fathers promised and John Wesley reminded us of.

## CONTINUAL SANCTIFICATION

*Even after "entire" sanctification, there is plenty of growth to come.* This has been the confusing thing about the term *entire sanctification* in recent decades. The word *entire* has come to connote "nothing more can be added." Yet, we realize we can be entirely in love with our spouse and still have room to grow!

So it is with our relationship with God. God can make us fully devoted followers of Jesus Christ, yet we still can have room to become more fully formed. Even should every sin be gone from our lives, there still is much room for increasing the *quality and amount* of our compassion, tenderness, and love. We may have the same kind of mercy Jesus Christ had but not express it continuously, as he did. Like the annual growth rings of a tree, there is much yet to put on. This is called *continual sanctification*. It is the ongoing work in the life of a fully *devoted* follower of Jesus, transforming him or her into the fully *formed* follower of Jesus Christ. Full devotion leads to full formation.

## GLORIFICATION

*At death the work of sanctification will be completed.* In glorification, God will finish the work not completed here on earth. Some have theorized that this happens in a purgatory, but there is scant biblical support for that. We know that when we see him we shall be like him. Whatever is in our life at death that does not belong in heaven will be finally and completely cleansed between our death and the moment we face Christ. Whether we are a brand-new Christian struggling with shameful habits or an entirely sanctified Christian widely known to be a saint, God will finish his work in us before we meet him face to face.

## DECLINING EMPHASIS ON ENTIRE SANCTIFICATION

*Not much is said about entire sanctification today.* This is true even within the denominations of the Holiness Movement and United Methodists, all of whom have strong statements about it in their church manuals or disciplines. When most folk today hear about entire sanctification, they say, "I think I'll choose the progressive one; that makes the most sense to me." Scan today's popular books or listen in on Sunday school class discussions, and progressive sanctification is all you'll hear. Entire sanctification is out of style.

*It is no wonder.* Entire sanctification is a confusing term. "Entire" is like "perfect," hard words for us ever to say about ourselves.

Moreover, there have been abuses in the past with people claiming to be "holiness people" who refused to drink, smoke, or attend movies, but who exhibited totally putrid attitudes and treated others dreadfully. In addition, we in the Holiness Movement rejected the Charismatic Movement so soundly, we sometimes became suspicious of ideas like "deliverance" or too much emphasis on the Holy Spirit. Finally, when the Holiness Movement married evangelicalism, we downplayed our own family traditions for the sake of the marriage.

Holiness people once had a mission of spreading *Christian holiness* mostly to other believers—people in mainline churches who already were saved. We were something like a parachurch organization, committed to helping other Christians find total victory over sin. Over time, our primary mission became evangelistic—getting people saved initially. This is not bad, just different. We have already mentioned our Western culture of evangelical gradualism, in which preaching any instantaneous change makes the preacher sound wacky. For all these reasons (and others), a whole generation of Christians arose who say they have never heard of this idea and have never heard a real person testify to the experience.

One preacher said, "It is like preaching on healing: They believe it might be theoretically possible, but they doubt it ever happens in real life." This preacher also said, "When I preach on entire sanctification, it is completely rejected by almost all of my people and reduces my credibility in other areas."

With today's cultural values of authenticity, one must confess some secret sin to be considered "authentic." Confessing to deliverance from sin or to holiness makes a person look like he or she is bragging. Confessing addiction to pornography will get an audience before confessing to entire sanctification. But besides all these factors, there is an even more important one: the popularity of sin. Some may cling to their progressive sanctification because they want to believe it will allow them to keep on practicing favorite sins, while pretending to be gradually recovering.

## PROCLAIMING HOLINESS IN AN ERA OF UNBELIEF

So what does a preacher do if he or she believes God really can cleanse and empower Christians through entire sanctification? How does a preacher keep from being run out of town, or from losing all credibility, while being faithful to this truth?

*We preach life-changing conversion.* The great risk today is not losing life-changing sanctification—it is losing life-changing conversion. So we preach about real change in real people at initial sanctification. Conversion is more than a decision to accept Christ, to follow Christ, or to start a new life. It is a life-changing experience of God's grace. So we preach it that way. We expect life change when people are saved, and we have them tell about it when they are baptized. We *can* and *should* preach life change in conversion—that powerful act of God that changes who we are and delivers us from sin. Preaching life-changing conversion builds faith in God's power to change people.

*We preach progressive holiness.* In today's culture, ninety percent of our preaching on holiness probably should focus on progressive sanctification. So we preach convicting sermons on specific sins and specific virtues, expecting our hearers to be convicted by the Spirit, then to respond and seek God's deliverance. If a Christian never has been delivered from a particular sin, or empowered to live a particular virtue, how could he or she ever believe it is possible to be *entirely* sanctified? So we preach convicting sermons that call for God's changing grace.

*We encourage testimonies.* If a tree falls in the woods and nobody is there, the question of whether there is sound is pointless. Likewise, if people are being delivered and changed in our church, but nobody hears about it, the miracle is useless to most of the fellowship. Because of past abuses, and perhaps because we who are the clergy don't want to risk losing control of "our" services, use of the testimony has declined in most churches. Yet in today's narrative culture, a testimony has more power than most sermons. When people hear the testimony of a new convert who has been delivered from alcohol or drugs, or from cheating on income taxes, or from being a cranky spouse, it puts flesh on our sermons. When a person has been changed, the church needs to hear about it. It builds faith in God's power to change. It turns an atmosphere of unbelief into one of faith and expectation.

*People's faith for deliverance increases.* As people hear preaching on life change, as some respond and testify to God's deliverance and empowering, the rest of the congregation begins to expect life change too. They begin to believe this church is "a place where God changes lives." They come expectantly and hopefully. When the Spirit nudges them about their own needs they do not despair, but hope for deliverance and power. When people hear public testimonies in worship about real life-change in real people, they start to share their own life changes in smaller settings—in Sunday school, in small groups, and over lunch.

Gradually the local church becomes a gathering of people who experience God's life-changing power. The church gathered becomes a people and a place of expectancy, an occasion where God's grace flows. Soon we become a place where people are not just *forgiven* of sins but also are *delivered* from sin by God's power. We become a church that not only talks about Christ's virtues, but also testifies, individually and corporately, to receiving the power and grace actually to live like this. God's work among us becomes great, and people expect him to work.

*We preach becoming "fully devoted followers of Jesus Christ."* In this sort of atmosphere, we easily can preach the positive possibility of being *fully* devoted. To those who are only "playing the Christian game," it may seem preposterous. But to those in the atmosphere described above, it seems completely logical: "If God is in the life-changing business here, why would he not be able to change me more than I ever thought?" Preaching holiness to the Christian game-players brings rejection. Preaching holiness to people who have been constantly changing through God's power brings spiritual revival. "Why didn't someone tell me this before?" they will say. Of course, we did tell them, but they did not hear it. Once they experienced a community where people constantly are being changed by God, they could hear it and believe it.

*Some will experience entire sanctification.* In this atmosphere, sooner or later some will be entirely sanctified. And they will talk about it. We will begin to have a church packed with people who are sensitive to the prompting of the Holy Spirit, who have been and are being changed by God's power. Perhaps we ourselves will experience it even after preaching to others. We *can* have this kind of church, if we don't have it now.

And what would we call that kind of church? Well, that would be a "holiness church."

## REFLECTION/ACTION SUGGESTIONS

**1.** Think about our "Western culture of gradualism" and its effect on the evangelical church. What other effects does it have on us? Write down some of your observations and conclusions, and discuss them with a mentor or peer in ministry.

**2.** God sometimes changes a person through wholly "spiritual" means, while at other times God uses human help. Can you recall times when God used each of these means to bring about change in your own life? Tell someone about it, in a personal conversation, or even in a sermon.

**3.** Some old-timers used to say, "Preach entire sanctification, and everything else will take care of itself." This chapter suggests a different approach in an era of unbelief. Is there any truth to the old-timers' statement? If so, what?

# PRACTICAL HOLINESS

*Judy Huffman*

*Until we all reach unity . . . and become mature, attaining to the whole measure of the fullness of Christ.*

—Ephesians 4:12–13

*Holiness is . . . haveable for the ordinary people of our day. It is possible for common people to have an uncommon love for God. It is possible to do what is right and like it. . . . It is possible to really know we are pleasing God. This is the sanctified life. This is the meaning of holiness.*

—Steve DeNeff

A while ago, I got a lamb's wool sweater at a yard sale for two dollars. It is the softest fabric around, far finer than cashmere or fluffy fleece. When I wear it funny things happen. Last month at a professional conference, six different strangers walked up to me within one morning and touched my sweater. They said things like, "I can't help myself; I just have to feel this."

True holiness is like that. True holiness draws people, because they long to experience the comfort and care of the Lamb of God's perfect love. The more we "wear" his grace, the more others will be drawn to him through us, and the more we will be drawn to one another. In this chapter we will focus on the relational aspect of holiness.

## HOLINESS: THE GREAT DIVIDE

In the mid-twentieth century, the first- and second-generation fervor over what we may call the "second rediscovery" of holiness as a biblical mandate and privilege began to ebb, though it did not disappear completely. As it ebbed, it was partially replaced by an emphasis on living out holiness externally with what could be called "perfect actions." Binding "church rules" became a major focus, replacing or being seen as proof of inner holiness. These included the familiar do's: do wear long sleeves, do wear short hair (men), do make sure your dresses cover your knees (women); and the familiar don'ts: for women—don't wear jewelry, don't wear makeup, don't wear pants; and for everyone—don't dance, don't play cards, don't watch TV.

By the mid-1960s, these so-called holiness standards became the focus of controversy. Some held tenaciously to them, honestly believing these behaviors were the marks of obedience to the Spirit of God and a surrendered life. Others experimented, found God still loving them after the rules were broken, and left the church rather than bear the ridicule dished out by "holy ones." Sadly, for another group what was called holiness became for them a repelling force, and they moved away, both from the church and from God.

But some people lived in the middle of the controversy and didn't really know what to do. Even while questioning the validity of these rules, they found some comfort in them. If all one had to do was follow a certain set of guidelines, then it was fairly easy to be a holy person. Granted, you had to be socially odd, but your acceptance came from the church world, and they held you up as virtuous. So being odd was not that big a deal.

My own understanding of this struggle turned a corner when I was twenty. I was traveling with my brother and sister-in-law; Jim and Judith were thirteen years older than I. They were bright, intelligent, godly mentors for me. Their age, their love for me, and their diligent pursuit of God gave them profound influence in my life. As we rode together, the holiness controversy made its way into our discussion, and Judith made a radical statement. She said she believed many Wesleyans were lazy in their faith, relying on rules rather than seeking to know and apply God's principles to daily life. She cited multiple examples of how individuals treated others cruelly in the name of holiness, for the protection of church rules.

I was hurt and offended, because I could follow rules easily, and I really wanted to be holy. Also, I felt a need to defend the "holy righteous" even though I immediately sensed she was right. Judith knew merely following the rules was not enough and that holiness has more to do with how we treat others than with being loyal to a list of rules. I was appalled by her heresy and frightened by her truth.

Not yet understanding the broader and deeper potential of holiness, I put the language of holiness away. Indeed, I became rather ashamed of holiness. I was not alone.

Throughout the next thirty years, God used his people to bring me back to his mystery of holiness, and he allowed The Wesleyan Church to be part of that process. Keith Drury, Jo Anne Lyon, Steve DeNeff, Ken Schenck, Melvin Dieter, and many others engaged in open exploration; they studied Scripture, learned from masters of old, and reopened the door to holiness. By refining the definition of holiness as a full and complete transformation of nature that enables every believer to be holy, they held on to the belief in Christian perfection. But they also acknowledged the full work of holiness as far more than a set of rules dictating external behaviors.

This honest approach makes it possible for believers to set their sights high, expecting that a biblical perfection can come in this lifetime through the work of the Holy Spirit. But it is no longer necessary to hide sin, for fear it will challenge a doctrinal position. Thanks to this new understanding of God's unchanging truth, our theologians have reopened the hope found in holiness. Now, in community, believers can lovingly assist each other in spiritual struggles. Rather than needing to "act right at all times," we strive to love with the perfect and full love of God, knowing that right actions will be born out of full love.

This shift brings us to a practical approach to holiness I call relational holiness: human wholeness born out of God's perfect love, which transforms us so we can love God and others with his divine love. In this process we become who God designed us to be, fully human and fully partnered, at God's invitation, into intimate family relationship with the Trinity.

## RELATIONAL HOLINESS AS FOUND IN EPHESIANS

Wesleyans understand that relational holiness is present and can be studied throughout the Bible. I have come to believe, though, that Paul's short letter to the Ephesians offers a compact summary of the whole. In Ephesians, I see Paul setting forth and discussing four components of relational holiness.

First, *the Triune God is the model of holiness—the Trinity is relational at its core*. The entire book of Ephesians is interwoven with the interdependent love within the Trinity. God, the Three in One, is our model of wholeness and holiness, our standard for "getting along."

Second, *God's love for us is the power of relational holiness*. Most dramatically, Jesus' death and resurrection combine with his life as the perfect visible expression of his love for us. From his resurrection love, we receive power to love.

Third, *relational holiness is characterized by God's offer to partner with humans*. We don't have to go it alone. We are given the Holy Spirit, who blesses individuals with gifts and graces for the specific purpose of building up the body of Christ together, in partnership.

Finally, we are called to rely on the power of his love and to have boldness in our partnership with him so we can *live well together* for his glory.

## OUR MODEL: THE TRIUNE GOD

To understand relational holiness rightly, it is essential to begin with the Triune God. Unlike other religions, Christianity is not the product of a one-dimensional sovereign. Neither is it defined by a god made up of competing personalities. The God of Christendom is three in one, relating together in love (see John 17:6–26; Eph.1:5–6; 4:4–6). It is because of this unified nature of God that relational holiness exists. God the Father's love for the Son is stated at the beginning of Ephesians: "In love he predestined us to be adopted as his sons through Jesus Christ, in accordance with his pleasure and will—to the praise of his glorious grace, which he has freely given us in the One he loves" (Eph. 1:4–6).

Later, Paul instructed us to "be imitators of God" (Eph. 5:1). In fact, he wrote this letter to remind believers that God calls us to love, unity, peace, and the empowerment of others. Those very qualities are revealed in the working relationship between God who is Father, Son, and Holy Spirit. We are told to imitate *God*, not "merely" Jesus at this point. We are to be one as God is one. This is the foundation of relational holiness, the assurance that interdependence is not only possible, it is essential.

A friend once told me the greatest compliment we can pay anyone is to need him or her. We see this expressed within the Trinity. God the Father entrusted Jesus with the earthly mission of restoration. The Holy Spirit was directed to be our Keeper after Jesus returned to heaven (Eph. 1:13–14). God the Father designated the flow of wisdom and revelation, but uses the Spirit to deliver these gifts (verse 17). While Jesus came to earth as an atonement for our sins, he relied on God the Father to raise him back to life (verse 20). God then appointed Jesus to be Head over everything for the Church (verse 22). In all this, there is no evidence of jealousy, competition, back-biting, or pouting. In the Trinity we see respect, confidence, full unity of heart and soul. In the Trinity, we are shown perfect love, the beginning point for relational holiness. God serves as the example of what he wants to restore in us!

## THE POWER: GOD'S LOVE FOR US

As I misunderstood it while growing up, holiness seemed to be oppressive, fearful, and focused on what I should be doing. This is a strong contrast to the relational side of holiness, which is marked by love, grace, and what God already has done for us! The language of Ephesians 1, describing God's love for his creation, is exuberant, even excessive: "blessed us . . . with every spiritual blessing" (verse 3); "he chose us . . . to be holy and blameless in his sight" (verse 4); "In love he predestined us to be adopted" (verses 4–5); "his glorious grace, which he has freely given us in the One he loves" (verse 6); "We have redemption . . . forgiveness of sins, in accordance with the riches of God's grace" (verse 7); "he lavished on us . . . according to his good pleasure" (verses 8–9).

God's opulent love makes it possible for us to be restored as fully human, restored to the complete image of God. God's love is the power that drives relational holiness. Without his love for us, it never would be possible for us truly to love others.

## THE ESSENCE: PARTNERSHIP WITH GOD

We are invited to take part in the interdependence that is evident in the Trinity. In love, God offers an invitation to partner with him. This is no small thing. Consider the young lawyer who signs on with a large law firm. She may work for years before being considered for a partnership. She has to prove herself, do the dirty work, and put in long hours. Then, maybe, she will be invited in as a partner. Or maybe, even after she has given her all to the firm, someone else will be chosen. She has no assurance her hard work will pay off.

Contrast this with God's invitation, made while we still are sinners. In God's partnership, it is not about us or our hard work; rather, it is because of who God is that we are invited. God's grace gives us a place at the table.

This partnership has two dimensions. First, it is a partnership between God and the entire collection of God's people, the Church (Eph. 3:10). In the Church, people are given gifts and graces "to prepare God's people for works of service, so that the body of Christ may be built up until we all reach unity . . . and become mature, attaining to the whole measure of the fullness of Christ" (4:12–13). God gives the Church unique authority and responsibility that, collectively, we may work with him to reclaim his world.

Keith Drury describes this partnership well in *There is No I in Church.* He challenges today's individualistic approach to knowing and worshiping God. With courage and wisdom, Drury tackles the narcissism that has crept into the Church. He calls Christians back to an elevated understanding of the Church as God's bride, one of his primary tools of restoration. The partnership between God and the Church is one dimension of relational holiness.

The other dimension is the smaller partnerships that make up the whole of the Church, for God partners with us individually as well as corporately. At this level relational holiness stands firmly as the hope for healthy relationships. God's design is not merely for a changed world, but also for changed lives. In this partnership God offers himself, his love, the power of Christ Jesus, and the presence of the Holy Spirit. We offer ourselves. It seems God gives far more than he asks, and that is true. This truth changes holiness from the dreaded "holiness list" to obedience and submission overflowing from love and trust. In relational holiness there is a transformation from "do's and don'ts" to the honor of *serving with God* and the mystery of what that will look like each day.

## THE END: LIVING WELL TOGETHER

The final component of relational holiness is the one that hits us most directly: living well together. Whether you are six or ninety-six, single or married, retired or climbing some invisible ladder, this is about you. God's call to live together in peace and unity may be his toughest call. So, in his grace, God gives us some principles to help along the way.

The first principle, *acquiring a divine view of others*, may be the most important. When this one is working, all the other principles are easier to embrace. We need the Spirit to help us see others as God sees all of us: "holy and blameless in his sight" (Eph. 1:4). This means we look past their current condition and see them as God created them to be. Sadly, the further humanity has distanced itself from the one true human, Jesus Christ, the further we have distanced ourselves from each other. The way to unity is through Christ, and that begins by acquiring his divine view.

This directive comes to us in Ephesians 4:2, where we are instructed to "be completely humble and gentle; be patient, bearing with one another in love." Humility comes first, and it is recognizing that everyone is created in God's image, and each one has something worth seeing and discovering. Humility is not about putting oneself down; it is about realizing that every person is made in the image of God. Humility reminds us that, because of God's partnerships with humans, we have reason to respect and value each person we meet. Humility reminds me that whether these persons are like me or different from me, they have insights, gifts, and graces to share with me, and I with them. Even those who are the greatest distance from Christ deserve my love. If I see them with his eyes, I see their true worth; and I am allowed to be a part of his work of redemption and restoration (1:14–22). This is a divine perspective.

*Relationships have eternal purpose and meaning.* This second principle moves us beyond our view of others to our understanding of relationships. This principle is true of the relational power of the Church as a whole, and God shows up even in each relationship of two or more persons. It was the relationship of Father and Son that made Christ's sacrifice powerful enough to claim our redemption (Eph. 1:4–7; 2:4–8). It is through the relationship of the Father and the Holy Spirit that we are kept, and through which we have access to the Father (2:18, 22). It stands to reason that God's relationship with us is eternal, because God is eternal; therefore, anything or anyone God brings to himself takes on an eternal dimension.

In addition, the divine nature of relationships is passed on to us. Contrary to contemporary culture's portrayal of relationships as self-gratifying and transient, God designed relationships for mutual respect (Eph. 5:1–2; 5:21—6:9) and shared purpose (1:19–22; 4:3, 11–16), and he set this in an eternal context (3:10–12). Relational holiness is the hope that God can work in and through all the relationships of our life, because they were designed for far more than we can see or imagine. Relationships are God's tool to accomplish divine purposes.

The third principle—we are to *commit ourselves to thoughts, words, and behaviors that serve and edify others*—gets to the heart of daily living. Notice the comprehensive breadth of this challenge. It begins with our minds (Eph. 4:17–24). What we think about directly influences the quality of our relationships. Next it moves to what we say to one another (4:29–30; 5:6–7, 19–20). The call is to edify and build each other up with our words. This is not flattery. On the contrary, we are called to speak the truth in love (4:15, 25).

Neither is it merely about "not lying"; it is about being courageous enough to be honest. Additionally, our behaviors are to reflect the love seen in the Trinity (Eph. 4–5).

Finally, *we are to rely on the power and enabling of God.* This last principle for living well together is a bookend of the first, that is, taking the Trinity as our model of relational holiness. Ephesians 6:10–18 encourages us to put on the full armor of God. How interesting that this comes after chapters of discussion regarding getting along. Is it possible that the armor of God is there to help us find wholeness in relationships?

Starting with God's character as "three perfectly coexisting as one" and ending with his presence dwelling within us, we see how we have hope for healthy relationships. Never for a moment do we need to do this in our own strength or wisdom. Because of God the Three-in-One we truly can live lives of peace and love. Moreover, in learning to live rightly in relationships we are being formed more fully into God's image.

## SPIRITUAL DISCIPLINES: LIGHTS ALONG THE ROAD

On the road to relational holiness, the practice of spiritual disciplines has stood as a shining beacon throughout the last three decades. In 1978, Richard Foster resurrected the classic disciplines in his *Celebration of Discipline*. This book exerted a powerful corrective pull within the Church. Rather than focusing on the legalistic list, Foster returned to the essentials of faith across the centuries. He called for behaviors to restore the inner life, enlist in outward service, and deepen faith expressed in community. Without Foster's talking about holiness, God used Foster's writings to help us become more like Christ. In this, he balanced personal piety with life in community. It is not merely what people do; equally important is how we live with one another.

The value and holistic nature of the disciplines is evident in the frequency with which they continue to show up in church literature. Foster was followed by Keith Drury in 1989. Drury's *Disciplines of Holy Living* introduced practices particularly salient for people who had grown up in The Wesleyan Church. Drury included restitution, forgiveness, and restoring the fallen Christian—valuable qualities for people recovering from legalism. These qualities highlight the relational nature of holiness.

In 1991, Donald Whitney published *Spiritual Disciplines for the Christian Life*. This work paralleled Foster quite closely, but added the disciplines of journaling and evangelism. In *The Life You've Always Wanted*, published in 2002, John Ortberg introduced the culturally sensitive discipline of "slowing," a discipline that impacts relationships with God and others. Finally, in 2005 Drury's highly practical work, *With Unveiled Faces*, reintroduced the primary disciplines from Foster's work and added the timely traits of rest and hospitality.

An overview of these five approaches reveals two particularly salient values for developing relational holiness. One is that practicing the disciplines puts us in a posture to hear from God. Since God is infinite and we are finite, we need help getting our minds around the Great One. True, we have been given the Holy Spirit, but he does not force himself on us. Through the disciplines of solitude, prayer, study, and rest we quiet ourselves in his presence. In his presence we find grace and understand his love. As we engage in the disciplines, we are brought into an intimate relationship with God. Since our relationship with him is the heart and soul of every other relationship, this is the starting point of relational wholeness.

A second value is that the spiritual disciplines specifically turned a light on the role of community in spiritual formation. All four authors (five books) incorporated forms of communal disciplines. This emphasis on community strengthened a relational holiness even when the church was not talking much about it.

## RELATIONAL HOLINESS, PRACTICALLY SPEAKING

Relational holiness is an aspect of holiness that acknowledges the importance of relationships in two ways. First, it is through relationships that God transforms us. Second, as we grow in holiness, our relationships are transformed: We will love better, and thus our relationships will become more pleasing to God and others. This in no way negates the importance of the spiritual disciplines as a practical demonstration of holiness; it is merely another angle of understanding.

I would go so far as to suggest that holiness that does not show up in our relationships is not truly holiness. Equally, holiness is not possible without community life, without the church. Nothing in all of Scripture allows for a life lived in isolation. On the contrary, from Genesis through Revelation, the Bible is a book of love, a book of connection, a book of struggle for intimacy between God and his people. If holiness is the restoration of each one into full humanity, then holiness is the restoration of relationships!

## RELATIONAL HOLINESS FOR THIS DAY

As I sat working on this chapter, a friend and great "doer of good" drove his van up to my office window and waved. I knew he was going to pick up volunteers for the community clean-up day. My immediate thought was that his actions were far more holy than my activity of writing about holiness. But were they?

The measure of holiness can't be determined by a gradient to-do list. Instead, holiness is becoming more and more of who God created us to be. As we grow in holiness, we grow in our love for God and others. What holiness looks like in day-to-day life varies. But the presence or absence of holiness will always impact relationships. As God is forming us into the persons he created us to be, our ability to love well will grow. Our understanding of what love looks like in relationships will deepen.

So for today, my friend Jack's act of relational holiness is to go help clean up the city. But my act of love for today is to be faithful—to keep my word and meet a deadline. For me, for today, relational holiness is studying, thinking, praying, writing—and, of course, resting in the holiness of God, in his perfect love.

## ACTION/REFLECTION SUGGESTIONS

**1.** If you are interested in thinking more about the idea of relational holiness, I encourage you to study Ephesians. Read through the entire book in one sitting to catch the tone. Then go back and mark every component of the chapter that is based on a relationship, keeping track of three different relationships: (1) God relating to and within his triune nature; (2) God relating to people; (3) people relating to people. Notice the connections between relationships and holy living. As you study, make this more than an academic exercise; consistently invite God to reveal himself and his design for us, his much-loved children.

**2.** Develop a divine view of your "problem" person. Consider one person in your life who is hard to respect or like. Begin to pray every day for that person, inviting God to help you to see this difficult person as God sees him or her. Ask yourself these questions:

- **a.** What is God doing in this person's life?
- **b.** How am I to be a part of God's work of love and transformation in and for this person?
- **c.** What am I to learn from this person?

**3.** Speak truth. It is far easier to fuss about people than to deal honestly with them. Are you upset with anyone in your life? What are you doing about that? Prayerfully consider what needs to be said. Talk with a friend who will help you practice what you need to say. Pray for a right time to talk with the person. Ask your friend to pray for the time of truth telling. When it is time, remember to speak truth in a context of listening.

10

# SOCIAL HOLINESS

*Robert Black*

*Consequently, you are no longer foreigners and aliens, but fellow citizens with God's people and members of God's household, built on the foundation of the apostles and prophets, with Christ Jesus himself as the chief cornerstone. In him the whole building is joined together and rises to become a holy temple in the Lord. And in him you too are being built together to become a dwelling in which God lives by his Spirit.*

—Ephesians 2:19–22

*There is no holiness but social holiness.*

—John Wesley

Simon Stylites was a fifth-century monk who sought holiness in the solitude of the Syrian Desert, miles from civilization. The world was corrupt, he reasoned, and if he remained in contact with the world, it could corrupt him. He was convinced the best way to express his attachment to God was by his detachment from society.

Reports of his piety circulated, however, and pilgrims sought him out for prayer and spiritual counsel. Simon's response was to build a platform on a stone pillar thirteen feet above the desert floor. For years he lived on that platform, exposed to wind and weather, seeking the solitude he treasured. But solitude is difficult for a celebrity, and Simon definitely had become a celebrity. When word of his unusual lifestyle began to spread, sightseers came in increasing numbers; the hermit had become a tourist attraction. He built a taller pillar, and an even taller one after that. Over the years his platform was raised by stages until, at the end of his life almost four decades later, it rose more than fifty feet above the desert floor, and the eccentric monk on top of it was more famous than ever. (To his credit, St. Simon did speak every afternoon with all who made the pilgrimage to his pillar, and God no doubt brought good out of what we would consider a bizarre choice.)

Simon knew that sanctification means to be set apart for God's use. If the concept of *separation* is key, then separation from a sinful world (and a disappointing church) while committing to a highly ascetic lifestyle must be the highest good, he thought. Not so, if we listen to Christ. His formula for holiness was "in the world but not of the world" (John 17:13–19), separation from sin not separation from society, insulation not isolation.

John Wesley had the highest regard for the "primitive" (early) church, but he couldn't understand fifth-century Christian hermits any more than he could understand the reclusive Christian mystics of his day. "Solitary religion is not to be found [in the gospel]," Wesley wrote just a year after his Aldersgate experience. "'Holy solitaries' is a phrase no more consistent with the gospel than holy adulterers. The gospel of Christ knows of no religion but social, no holiness but social holiness."

## A TRADITION OF PERSONAL HOLINESS

Simon Stylites was not wrong to pursue personal holiness. Devout Christians always have. Throughout its history the church can point to sterling examples of Christlikeness in the lives of countless men and women fully surrendered to the will and work of God in their hearts, and both the church and the world are better for it. Some have been world renowned; others are virtually unknown.

## TWO WHOM I HAVE KNOWN

Jim Teague was a leader in the church of my childhood. Even as a kid I knew "Uncle Jimmy" to be a man of God, but it was not until later that I learned his story. Back in 1916 when the young congregation was ready to build, funds were tight. The bank offered only a small loan, and it began to look like their dreams of a building would never be realized. At the time of their deepest discouragement, Jimmy Teague mortgaged his own home to help finance the construction of the new church. His friends warned him, "Jimmy, these are hard times. You could lose your home." He replied, "If I don't have a church, I don't need a home."

Years later, I was pastor to Elizabeth Bray, who bought a house on the city bus line when she retired. Every morning she rose at her regular time, but she went to work for God instead of for Blue Cross. Often she rode the bus to visit hospitals, nursing homes, and shut-ins all over Richmond, Virginia. She created her own "bus ministry" and poured herself into it year after year.

You probably don't know Jim Teague or Elizabeth Bray; neither became a household name. They're among the multitudes better known in heaven than on earth. Yet when I think of personal holiness, theirs are two of the faces I picture.

## AN ENDLESS LINE OF SPLENDOR

The Holiness Movement has produced men and women like that for nearly two centuries now—almost three, if you start the clock with Wesley's revival in England. A personal hunger for God has energized their spiritual quests, and they have known both the joy of the Spirit-filled life and the anticipation of an infinitely greater communion with God for all eternity. Holiness has been for them "a little bit of heaven to go to heaven in," as the saying goes.

Still it's important to note that the personal holiness of my two friends profoundly impacted others. Far from just filling a well to water their own souls, the Spirit flowed through them as a channel of blessing to others, both inside and outside the faith. Their legacies are far greater than the ruins of a pillar in the desert, because they are legacies of love.

And love is a social grace.

Howard Snyder put it this way: "Holiness, while personal, is not first of all *individual*. It is primarily *social*, as Wesley insisted."[1]

## A CALL TO SOCIAL HOLINESS

Social holiness operates on several levels, each with a biblical basis and a practical application. To be like their Lord, holiness Christians must have a heart for others, a zeal for social justice, and, ultimately, a sense of corporate holiness that transcends the personal holiness of individual believers.

### THE OUTWARDNESS OF HOLINESS

When pressed for a definition of holiness, Wesley turned to Christ's identification of the greatest commandment in Matthew 22: love God completely and love others as yourself. For Wesley love, "perfect love," is what holiness is all about. Love requires relationship. It's not a privatized experience. If it's turned inward, it withers. As Dennis Kinlaw maintains, "Outwardness is all there is to the gospel."[2]

Obviously, I need to live out that vertical relationship with God in my horizontal relationships with others. We understand relationships. Our lives are full of them. I'm a husband to my wife, a father to my children, a grandfather to my granddaughter, a son to my mother, a brother to my brother, a nephew to my aunt, and an uncle to my nephews and nieces. To the state, I'm a citizen. To the merchant, I'm a customer. To my students, I'm a teacher. To the patrolman, I'm a driver. I understand relationships, and when I see holiness as a deeper and fuller relationship with God in Christ through the Holy Spirit—a love relationship—I understand it better, too. Obviously, I need to live out this vertical relationship with God in my horizontal relationships with others.

Any holy lifestyle worth its salt (in the sense of Matt. 5:13) will show God's grace to others, because we are recipients of that same grace. We can love others precisely because we have come to know his love, and we can show others "perfect love" only when the One who loves them perfectly has been given to us (Luke 11:13).

We are never promised holiness, after all. We are promised the Holy Spirit (Luke 11:13; John 14:16–17; Gal. 3:5; Eph. 1:17), and the Spirit is a person, the third person of the Trinity, who desires an ever-deepening relationship with us. That relationship produces in us new attitudes that lead to new actions. Paul called it our "new self" (Eph. 4:22–24). To others it is the higher life, or the deeper life, or entire sanctification. To all, it is Christian holiness, and its hallmark is love.

"Love one another" (John 13:34, to cite just one of the thirteen occurrences of that exhortation in the New Testament) is one of the mutuality commands that sprinkle the Scripture and remind us of our interrelatedness. In fact, it's the *foundational* mutuality command, the spring from which all the others flow. We also are to be kind to one another (Eph. 4:32), to be devoted to one another (Rom. 12:10), to serve one another (Gal. 5:13), to submit to one another (Eph. 5:21), to carry one another's burdens (Gal. 6:2), to encourage one another (1 Thess. 5:11a), to build one another up (1 Thess. 5:11b), to bear with one another (Col. 3:13a), to forgive one another (Col. 3:13b), to admonish one another (Col. 3:16), to confess our sins to one another (James 5:16a), to pray for one another (James 5:16b), and to spur one another on toward love and good deeds (Heb. 10:24). Each of these could carry a footnote: "See '*Love one another*.'"

*Koinonia* is the New Testament word for those layers of engagement with each other in the church. Unfortunately, the common English translation, "fellowship," has been stripped of much of its meaning in our day; to us, it suggests mere socializing. But fellowship in the New Testament sense is far more significant than enjoying a fellowship dinner in a fellowship hall. It means Christians, motivated by love, investing in the lives of others, often at considerable cost to themselves in terms of time, money, comfort, and energy. First-century Christians shared no shallow notion of the body of Christ. They were to be there for one another as Christ had been there for them.

Sometimes that means standing up against systemic evil.

## SOCIAL JUSTICE

Systemic evil is a problem in every age. In 2006, Timothy Smith's *Revivalism and Social Reform* (1957) was voted one of "The Top 50 Books That Have Shaped Evangelicals." In this classic study, Smith demonstrated that evangelical Christians, particularly in the holiness tradition, were not, as their critics would later claim, too heavenly minded to be any earthly good. On the contrary, holiness Christians within Methodism, Wesleyan Methodism, Free Methodism, and other denominations and institutions were at the forefront of the fight against slavery, poverty, and injustice in the days before the American Civil War. They made a difference, not despite their holiness mind-set, but because of it.

In that, they followed Wesley's model. Wesley the evangelist was also Wesley the reformer, all in the name of Christ. He was an early opponent of slavery, calling for its abolition in a day when few seemed concerned. He championed the cause of the poor, creating interest-free loan funds, free medical services, and a jobs program that was far ahead of its time. He elevated the role of women, promoted humanitarian treatment of prisoners, and campaigned against distilleries in a nation addicted to gin. As a result, England experienced a revival that changed not only the church but society, as well.

This topic need not be explored in depth here; another chapter in this book deals with compassionate ministries and social justice. No treatment of social holiness would be complete, though, without at least a passing reference to social action, especially since holiness reformers have always seen their labors as logical extensions of their theology: The God who had transformed them could transform the social order, too.

We haven't done as well with that vision of justice and equity in our day, most would agree. We need to ask ourselves why.

But on the other end of the pendulum's swing, we cannot simply equate social holiness with social justice. Wesley didn't. While his famous quote about social holiness is often marshaled in the call to arms for social causes, it's clear in context that it actually refers to being the body of Christ. Wesley won't let us settle for the role of solitary Christian.

Come to think of it, we haven't done so well with being the body of Christ, either—at least not in its highest and most biblical form.

## CORPORATE HOLINESS

As Keith Drury has pointed out in *There Is No I in Church* and Ken Schenck has demonstrated in an unpublished monograph prepared for a theological symposium, our notion of the church falls far short of God's design for it. We tend to see the body of Christ as the sum total of the Christians who comprise it, when in reality it is far greater.

In evangelical circles we have emphasized the necessity of personal faith, and rightly so, but an unintended consequence is that we have devalued the corporate dimension of the gospel. Our songs are filled with first-person-singular testimonies of grace, but the absence of the classic hymn-language reminding us that God is "*our* help in ages past" and "*our* hope for years to come" means we're often out of balance. One could say we have a singular problem.

Throughout the New Testament are "you" passages addressed to the church, passages we tend to read as though they are singular and intended for the individual reader. In fact, most are plural; our confusion results from the failure of the English language to differentiate between second-person singular and second-person plural pronouns (except in the South!).

Nor are these plurals just aggregate plurals that really mean "all of you individual believers." Some of God's grandest promises are not addressed primarily to each of us individually, but to all of us as a group, and some of his greatest works are not designed for each of us alone, but for all of us together. The idea is not so much that we are *in* the church, like members of a club or a team; it's that we *are* the church in a marvelously mystical but profoundly practical way.

None of us would be surprised to hear that in 1 Corinthians 6 Paul reminded each believer, individually, that his body, individually, is the temple, individually, of the Holy Spirit. That's a classic Christian concept, and holiness preachers have perhaps made more use of it than anyone else. But many *would* be surprised to discover that three chapters earlier Paul addressed *all* the Corinthian Christians together, corporately, when he wrote, "Don't you know that you yourselves [plural] are God's temple [singular!] and that God's Spirit lives in you [plural]? If anyone destroys God's temple, God will destroy him; for God's temple is sacred, and you [plural] are that temple [singular]" (1 Cor. 3:16–17). No individual temples in this metaphor—just one temple of God, comprised of all the Corinthian Christians together, and God's Spirit lives in it. His Spirit dwells not only in individual believers but in the community of faith, which together they create. Ephesians 2:21–22 says the same thing in the same way.

Even more to the point for our purposes, Ken Schenck emphasizes that "that great verse of Wesleyanism, 1 Thessalonians 5:23, is plural in address: 'May the God of peace himself sanctify you [plural] completely and may your [plural] entire spirit and soul and body [singular in reference to the whole church] be kept blameless at the coming of our Lord Jesus Christ.' This verse applies first to the body of Christ as the whole assembly of believers at Thessalonica and then only secondarily to us as individuals."[3]

Social holiness, then, also means corporate holiness. The Spirit of God indwells, blesses, corrects, convicts, and guides congregations as well as persons.

Charles Wesley was on solid ground biblically and theologically when he employed plural pronouns in the signature hymn of the Wesleyan doctrine of Christian perfection, "Love Divine, All Loves Excelling." Read these words through the lens of corporate holiness:

Breathe, oh, breathe Thy loving Spirit Into ev'ry troubled breast!
Let us all in Thee inherit; Let us find that second rest.
Take away our bent to sinning; Alpha and Omega be,
End of faith as its Beginning; Set our hearts at liberty.
Finish then Thy new creation; Pure and spotless let us be.
Let us see Thy great salvation, Perfectly restored in Thee:
Changed from glory into glory, Till in heav'n we take our place,
Till we cast our crowns before Thee, Lost in wonder, love, and praise!

These are the plurals of perfect love.

## THE DIVINE BOTH/AND

It's the divine both/and. We know the wonder of salvation and sanctification on a personal level, and for that we will forever be lost in wonder, love, and praise. What many of us have missed far too long is what it means to be the body of Christ in a true community of faith, the beneficiaries of a corporate redemptive relationship in which his Spirit wants to sanctify the whole body of Christ together, as well as the individual persons who make it up.

Heaven knows (literally), the body of Christ can look rather imperfect, but God is at work. Along with his choice saints he finds a few of us—okay, a lot of us—still rough around the edges, but for all he has the same design; he wants us to look like his Son.

On a personal level, we've been telling the rest of the Christian community that for a long time. On a corporate level, it's what they've been trying to say to us in return.

Somehow, I think Jim Teague and Elizabeth Bray understood it all along.

## ACTION/REFLECTION SUGGESTIONS

**1.** As part of a personal spiritual inventory, give yourself a "*koinonia* audit." Some questions worth including:

> Do I ever speak with others in the church about spiritual things, or do I somehow settle for the superficial in all my conversations?
>
> How quick am I to build up a fellow Christ-follower (*spiritual construction*)?
>
> How quick am I to tear down a brother or sister (*spiritual demolition*)?
>
> Whose life have I invested myself in lately?
>
> Whose load have I helped to lift?
>
> Am I a good listener when someone just needs to talk?
>
> Those new people in church—have I gotten to know them?
>
> Am I staying in touch with students in our congregation who are away at college?

Do I reach out to those in the church who have lost a loved one, remembering them especially at the holiday season or on the anniversary of their loss?

Do I know the names of the children and teens in our church?

For whom am I praying?

**2.** Try a "social action audit," too. Check your activity level in such areas as help for the homeless, the poor, and the single-parent families around you; openness in reality, not just in rhetoric, to people of all races and ethnic backgrounds; taking responsibility to make your neighborhood cleaner, safer, and more healthy for all its residents; standing up for equity and justice in the spirit of Christ. Politics aside, ask the same kinds of questions on the national and global level. Look for ways to make a difference in society.

**3.** Pray for the Spirit to move on your congregation as a whole, not just the individual members of it. All the things you pray for in terms of your own spiritual growth—things that would make you a better Christian—pray for those things for the body of Christ, taken together. Pray for the Spirit to sanctify ____________ (fill in the name of your church). Finally, ask the Spirit how He wants you to help answer your own prayer.

## NOTES

1. Howard Snyder, "Holiness of Heart and Life in a Postmodern World," in *Grace and Holiness in a Changing World: A Wesleyan Proposal for Postmodern Ministry*, eds. Jeffrey E. Greenway and Joel B. Green (Nashville: Abingdon, 2007), 76.

2. Dennis Kinlaw, *The Mind of Christ* (Nappanee, Ind.: Evangel, 1998), 101.

3. Ken Schenck, "The Church and the Holy Spirit" (paper presented at The Wesleyan Church's doctrinal symposium titled "A Wesleyan View of the Church," Indianapolis, Ind.: June 1–2, 2007), 6. Author's scripture translation.

# HOLINESS AND JUSTICE

*Jo Anne Lyon*

*I can't stand your religious meetings. I'm fed up with your conferences and conventions. I want nothing to do with your religion projects, your pretentious slogans and goals. I'm sick of your fundraising schemes, your public relations and image making. I've had all I can take of your noisy ego-music. When was the last time you sang to me? Do you know what I want? I want justice—oceans of it. I want fairness—rivers of it. That's what I want. That's all I want.*

—Amos 5:21–24 (MSG)

*Holiness necessarily passes through the World of Action.*

—Dag Hammarskjöld

I first saw injustice at an early age. This was a term totally out of my five-year-old vocabulary and, I am sure, that of my pastor father as well. However, as I grew older I matched the experience with the word. Growing up in the segregated state of Oklahoma, I saw people of color only on rare occasions. One of those times was the weekly trash pick-up by a vivacious, hymn-singing, African-American woman. Every Wednesday morning I pressed my nose against the glass in our front door to see and hear this woman. I often asked my parents where she lived and whether we could visit her. Finally, my father capitulated and assured me that on a certain day we would drive there.

The day finally arrived, and as we drove to what then was known as "colored town" in Enid, Oklahoma, I was overwhelmed. Here the paved road ended and the dirt road began. My first response was asking why "they" did not have a paved road. My father really could not answer this question. I saw schools, churches, and homes that were referred to as shacks, small eating "joints," vegetables sold on the road—a world I had not known existed. Taking all this in, I asked my father why "these people" did not attend our church. He told me "they" had their own church.

These images never left my mind. As I grew older, I began to understand more clearly the terms "justice" and "injustice." But it was years before I discovered the biblical and theological understanding of justice, how this relates to holiness and, more, how it is integrated into the living of a holy life.

During the late 1960s, Dr. Paul Rees, son of one of the founders of the Pilgrim Holiness Church, wrote a very intriguing book titled *Don't Sleep Through the Revolution*. I was drawn to this book on several levels. First of all, I was hearing almost nothing from holiness writers regarding biblical justice in connection with the civil rights struggle. Second, I wanted to know how this connected with the sanctified life.

Frankly, I never had heard these two terms—sanctification and justice—in *any* type of relationship. Sanctification was a personal thing that made us more holy, individually, but really did not spill over into public policy. Sanctification, or holiness, was about personal morality, such as drinking, smoking, dancing, movies, and so forth. On the other hand, I noted those who were involved in the civil rights struggle almost never talked about evangelism and tended to eschew issues of personal piety. The chasm between the two fields of thought was filled with "spiritual" superiority, each toward the other.

## THE BIBLICAL MANDATE

One of the paths of my journey led me on a lifelong adventure of biblical exploration. An early discovery was that the words *justice* and *righteousness* (important aspects of holiness) often appear together in Hebrew parallelism. An example is the text at the beginning of this chapter, "Let justice (*mishpat*) roll down like waters, and righteousness (*tsedaqah*) like an ever-flowing stream" (Amos 5:24 RSV).

The Hebrew noun *mishpat* ("justice") appears 422 times in the Old Testament. *Tsedaqah* ("righteousness") appears 157 times; it often denotes the way things should be, the norm or the standard. These two concepts have a theocentric foundation. Psalm 7:11 refers to God as a "righteous judge." Psalm 72:1–2 exhorts, "Endow the king with your justice, O God, the royal son with your righteousness. He will judge your people in righteousness, your afflicted ones with justice." As we see in Deuteronomy 10:17–19 (compare also 1:17), human justice must be God's justice.

Not only were these words used for procedural justice (fair courts, no bribes, and so forth), but the prophets used these words to call for economic justice, as well. *Mishpat* (justice) occurs in Micah 6:8: "[God requires you] to act justly and to love mercy and to walk humbly with your God."

Another association of justice is with love. Deuteronomy 10:18 declares, "[God] defends the cause of [literally, "does justice (*mishpat*) for"] the fatherless and the widow, and loves the alien, giving him food and clothing." Another example is Isaiah 30:18: "Yet the LORD longs to be gracious to you; he rises to show you compassion. For the LORD is a God of justice."

As we move on to understand the full biblical implication of justice, we see it as not just helping people to live in their suffering and oppression, but to bring deliverance. Justice is frequently associated with *yasha/yeshua*, the most important Hebrew word for deliverance and salvation. One example is Psalm 76:9 (ed. trans.): "When God arose to establish justice [*mishpat*], to save [*hoshe'a*] all the oppressed of the earth." Certainly, this is similar to Isaiah 63:1, where God describes himself as "speaking in righteousness, mighty to save." This also parallels the command of Psalm 82:3–4 to "maintain the rights of the poor and oppressed. Rescue the weak and needy; deliver them from the hand of the wicked."

Hundreds of verses throughout Scripture show God's great concern and care for the poor. When I first began this journey of inquiry, for a time I thought God cared more for the poor than for the rich. Many of the texts castigate the rich over the poor. But with careful examination it became obvious the texts were condemning the rich *because* of their oppression of the poor, to gain and maintain their own wealth.

This was precisely the situation during the time of the prophet Amos. The rich were mixing worship and oppression of the poor—a stench in the nostrils of God. But another factor, not much discussed, was Israel's complacency as noted, for example, in Amos 6. Here, God shouted at them about their complacency, lamenting how they lay on their "beds inlaid with ivory," and consumed their elegant food and wine while listening to their personally composed music (verses 4–6). This lifestyle made them totally numb to the suffering around them. Note these words were directed to the people of God, *not* to pagans!

The destruction of Sodom and Gomorrah adds another layer to the odium of complacency. Here, the infamous sexual demand of the men of Sodom upon Lot's guests (Gen. 19:4–5) is so overwhelming one may miss the underlying unrighteousness that resulted in this type of living: "Now this was the sin of your sister Sodom: She and her daughters were arrogant, overfed and unconcerned; they did not help the poor and needy" (Ezek. 16:49).

Jesus' words in Matthew 25:31–46 give us pause regarding the last judgment and the criteria for entering heaven. Echoing his and our Lord, John put it very strongly in 1 John 3:17, saying that if we don't care for a needy brother or sister, God's love is not even in us. Again, these texts are for those walking in the Spirit, for God's people, not for unbelievers.

Holy living resulting in destruction of the systems that perpetuate evil is the call of God throughout human history. Jonathan Edwards saw this as a result of revival. Richard Lovelace summarized Edwards: "Experiences of renewal which are genuinely from the Holy Spirit are God-centered in character. . . . Most important, their end result is the performance of works of *mercy and justice*."[1]

## WESLEY'S AWAKENING TO JUSTICE ISSUES

John Wesley and George Whitefield were forced by the majority church of their time to take their preaching to the streets and fields. As they began to mix with the lower classes, the poor, and those on the margins of society, new areas of pastoral care and concern arose. They found their new converts working hard, but being exploited by their employers.

Even worse was the total disregard for poor children, compelled to work long and dangerous hours. In the coal mines, for instance, children were forced into the most abhorrent and dangerous places because their small hands could reach the coal veins adult hands could not. This, of course, caused many early deaths—if not from accident, then from disease or disability. No laws or policies regulated the workday or the workweek, and pay was at the whim of the employer. Inevitably, these children were denied education and a future.

Prompted by his understanding of the biblical call for justice, Wesley began to support fair prices; a living wage; and honest, healthy employment for all. One result was the birth of the British

Labor movement, heavily influenced in its beginnings by Wesley and his followers.[2] One wonders what would have happened to hundreds and thousands of children and adults all over Britain had not this systemic evil been thwarted.

## HOLINESS AND THE ABOLITION OF SLAVERY

Today, all Christians would agree one of the most heinous examples of systemic evil is human slavery. However, I always find it disturbing to remember how long it took believers to understand the evil of this system. Slavery had so ingrained itself into the culture, from the economic systems of government to the theology and practice of the church, that it had become a silent tragedy and sin, endorsed by all. Yet, in time, a "troubling of the waters" began to manifest itself in people's souls.

Richard Baxter, a seventeenth-century English Puritan church leader and theologian, in his *Christian Directory* condemned the slave trade as "one of the worst kinds of Thievery in the World," but did not object to Christians owning slaves if they took pains to bring the gospel to them.[3] George Fox, founder of the Quaker movement, wrote to his followers in Barbados in 1671, urging Quaker slaveholders to care for their slaves both in soul and body, and to release them after a stated number of years in service.[4] Other Christians urged legislation regulating the number of hours slaves had to work; still others urged that housing for slaves be improved.

The list of this type of social care is as long as the imaginations of the people who wanted to relieve the slaves' suffering in some manner. Yet it took years for leaders to respond. The Quakers introduced the first British parliamentary memorial dealing with slavery—in 1783, more than *one hundred years* after the stirrings in the heart of their founder, George Fox.

William Wilberforce, who championed the antislavery memorial in the British Parliament for many years until its passage, was converted in 1785, at the age of fourteen, under John Wesley's ministry. In 1787 he wrote in his diary, "God Almighty has set before me two great objects, the suppression of the slave trade and the reformation of manners."[5]

In 1774, Wesley had issued a pamphlet titled *Thoughts on Slavery*. Speaking directly to the slave-trader and to the slave-owner, he had declared, "All slavery is as irreconcilable to Justice as to Mercy."[6] It is no wonder, then, that one of the last letters Wesley wrote was to William Wilberforce, in February, 1791, encouraging him, "Go on, in the name of God and in the power of his might, till even American slavery (the vilest that ever saw the sun) shall vanish away before it."

Wesley continued: "Reading this morning a tract wrote by a poor African, I was particularly struck by that circumstance that a man who has a black skin, being wronged or outraged by a white man, can have no redress; it being a 'law in our colonies that the *oath* of a black against a white goes for nothing. What villainy is this?'"[7]

The slave trade was officially defeated in Britain in 1807, by a lopsided vote in the House of Commons, 283 to 16, with overwhelming accolades to Wilberforce. Implementation took longer. In 1833, slave owners in the British Empire were required to release their slaves within a year. In addition, the British treasury compensated the former slaves with a total of twenty million pounds. This has been noted by some historians as one of perhaps three or four totally righteous governmental acts in history!

It is important to note that hundreds of prayer groups were involved in this long struggle, adding to their prayers, as well, widespread boycotts of sugar, cotton, and other consumer goods that perpetuated slavery. The night of the final parliamentary vote, people all over England were united in prayer. The Clapham leaders, aristocrats, were the heart of the prayer movement, regularly spending three separate hours in prayer daily.[8]

I believe this is one of the great models of the combination of personal piety and work in public policy—the combination of holiness and justice lived out. Wellman J. Warner, in a 1930 study regarding the impact of Wesleyan perfectionism on early English industrial society, stated, "The experience of sanctification socialized the individual disposition and released in men the mystic power to make benevolent motives work."[9]

This same notion followed from the life and preaching of Charles G. Finney as he preached sanctification and freedom from sin in the United States leading up to the American Civil War. By the time that great conflict began, it was well accepted that the power of the sanctifying gospel would reconstruct society, and the social ills of poverty, slavery, greed, cruelty and oppression could be abolished.[10]

## OTHER AMERICAN ISSUES: "REMOVAL" AND SUFFRAGE

Yet other injustices, other systems of evil, were perpetrated during these days, as well. In the 1830s, the U.S. government began to remove Native Americans forcibly from their homelands in the south. The most famous case is that of the Cherokee Nation, a strong, cohesive group of landowners and farmers, with their own schools, stores, and governance. (Ironically, some of the Cherokee even owned black slaves.)

Evangelical missionaries fought for the rights of the Native Americans. One in particular was Jeremiah Evarts, who organized petitions to Congress. Evarts argued, "The Cherokees are human beings endowed by their Creator with the same natural rights as other men."[11] Evarts and others worked for a decade—unsuccessfully. Some ministers who worked with him were harassed and jailed, but they were willing to raise their voices in protest and risk their lives in what was considered a criminal act against the American government. It was more important to obey God than human authority.

Daniel Wise, editor of *Zion's Herald*, a Methodist magazine in Boston, was an ardent promoter of scriptural holiness. He declared in one of his editorials, "Political action is moral action because the Lord expects our every act to be holy; to withdraw from politics is to encourage the growth of evil in the world."[12]

Parallel to the slavery issue in America in the nineteenth century was the issue of women's rights, focused then on securing "suffrage," the right to vote. It is astonishing in this day to realize women were not granted the right to vote until 1920. The battle for women to be seen as created in the image of God proved to be very long, indeed. In March, 1776, Abigail Adams had been so bold as to write her husband, John, as the men of the Continental Congress were debating the issue of independence from Britain, "Remember the Ladies." John responded with humor. The wording of the Declaration of Independence, adopted July 2 of that year, specifies "all *men* are created equal."

Again, in this battle for justice for women, the Wesleyan Holiness Movement led the way. Luther Lee, one of the founders of The Wesleyan Methodist Church, preached the sermon for the ordination of the first woman in America, Antoinette Brown; his text was Galatians 3:28. However, many sermons in defense of women in leadership in ministry stemmed from the prophecy of Joel as repeated by Peter at Pentecost. Seth Rees, one of the founders of the Pilgrim Holiness Church, wrote, "Sisters, let the Holy Ghost fill, call and anoint you to preach the glorious Gospel of our Lord."[13]

## WHERE WERE WE?

I return to my questions posed at the beginning of this chapter regarding holiness people and the civil rights movement. Where were we? The Wesleyan Methodist and Pilgrim Holiness churches merged in 1968. Dr. Virgil Mitchell, who was elected general superintendent at the merging general conference and served in that capacity for sixteen years, lamented before his death in 2006 that there was no mention in the proceedings of the 1968 conference of the burning struggles of injustice engulfing our culture at that time. He went on to say this omission was evidence of our isolation for a decade and he prayed it would never happen again.[14]

Where were we? In mistaken reaction against the "social gospel," we had abandoned our original leadership in the area of justice.

## WHERE DO WE GO FROM HERE?

As we look at our world in the current global context, we again (or still) are faced with issues of oppression that call for structural change to achieve the long-term justice God yearns to see. Following is a sample of structural changes we need to address, while at the same time working to alleviate suffering and evangelize the lost:

- AIDS prevention demands structural change in many countries, leading to equal status and opportunity for women, including the right to own land. In addition, those currently suffering from AIDS need greater access to treatment and care.
- Addressing twenty-first-century human trafficking demands laws in many more countries, making it a crime. In addition, the systems that create demand for this evil must be addressed—including greed, pornography, and the low value placed on the lives of women and children.

- Working to end hunger includes global fair trade, addressing consumption issues and growing consumerist mentalities, pushing for legislation in Western countries to help alleviate world hunger, and learning to become advocates for the hungry.
- Working to alleviate poverty means creating opportunities for work for the poor to support themselves, creating access to education and to fair legal systems, and advocating for legislation to lessen, or even remove, the oppression of the poor.
- Immigration is as much a hot-button issue now as slavery was in the nineteenth century. Just as did slavery, immigration carries its own set of structural issues to be addressed, if we are to deal with this problem holistically and justly.
- The questions of institutionalized racism, classism, sexism, and ageism overlie and color many of these issues, as well, aggravating our tendencies to hide or to justify. We must ask ourselves whether they *can* be hidden or justified, in light of Scripture, and in the presence of a fair and just God.
- Creation care, the sanctity of human life, protection of the institution of marriage, and religious freedom are issues begging for the voice of holiness and justice in the twenty-first century.

It is easy to feel overwhelmed and say, "Well, I'm just going to choose one issue." Or to say, "I'm just going to help people and leave the structural change to someone else, because I really don't get all this complexity." But we really do not have the luxury of choosing from a menu. Rather, we must learn again to see holiness and justice as a whole, which is what "living out holiness as a whole" really means.

This may mean tutoring a child whose parents are in prison, and at the same time working on prison reform. It may mean teaching English as a second language to an illegal immigrant, and at the same time working on laws that will enable him or her to find a pathway to citizenship. Meanwhile, we are to envelop all this in the love of Christ shared with the recipients of our services at the one-to-one level, as well as to evangelize those we encounter working at the structural level. History bears out that the Great Awakenings of the eighteenth and nineteenth centuries had their seeds in such settings.

Dr. Ellsworth Kalas said, "To be *sanctified* means to be ultimately serious about God and everything that relates to God (that is, *everything*)." He went on to say that "love sees things in life and in people that others never see, and that we really can't see until the baptism of love transforms our vision."[15]

## A PARABLE OF HOLY JUSTICE

A parable written by Ron Sider points out the layers of justification that many times cement our systems in place and blind us to the reality of structural sin.

> A group of devout Christians once lived in a small village at the foot of a mountain. A winding, slippery road with hairpin curves and steep precipices without guard rails wound its way up one side of the mountain and down the other. There were frequent fatal accidents. Deeply saddened by the injured people who were pulled from the wrecked cars, the Christians in the village's three churches decided to act. They pooled their resources and purchased an ambulance so that they could rush the injured to the hospital in the next town. Week after week church volunteers gave faithfully, even sacrificially, of their time to operate the ambulance

twenty-four hours a day. They saved many lives although some victims remained crippled for life.

Then one day a visitor came to town. Puzzled, he asked why they did not close the road over the mountain and build a tunnel instead. Startled at first, the ambulance volunteers quickly pointed out that this approach (although technically quite possible) was not realistic or advisable. After all, the narrow mountain road had been there for a long time. Besides, the mayor would bitterly oppose the idea. (He owned a large restaurant and service station halfway up the mountain.)

The visitor was shocked that the mayor's economic interests mattered more to these Christians than the many human casualties. Somewhat hesitantly, he suggested that perhaps the churches ought to speak to the mayor. After all, he was an elder in the oldest church in town. Perhaps they should even elect a different mayor if he proved stubborn and unconcerned. Now the Christians were shocked. With rising indignation and righteous conviction they informed the young radical that the church dare not become involved in politics. The church is called to preach the gospel and give a cup of cold water. Its mission is not to dabble in worldly things like social and political structures.

Perplexed and bitter, the visitor left. As he wandered out of the village, one question churned round and round in his muddled mind. Is it really more spiritual, he wondered, to operate the ambulances which pick up the bloody victims of destructive social structures than to try to change the structures themselves?[16]

## ACTION/REFLECTION SUGGESTIONS

**1.** Consider the allegory at the end of the chapter, reflect on current issues with which you are familiar, and make an application of the allegory to one issue. What keeps this issue from being resolved? What key systemic structures need to be changed to resolve it? How can you and your congregation begin to precipitate those changes?

**2.** From your everyday life, begin to take note of the justice issues that surround you continually. Where and how can you live out holiness in action?

**3.** Review your prayer journal. Do you pray for divine intervention and deliverance regarding contemporary issues? I believe many times we talk about, debate, and politicize these issues, but do not pray or expect miracles. What about your public prayers? Do they reach beyond the personal lives of the congregation? Most public prayer requests tend to be about the health of the congregants. Be bold and reach beyond those boundaries. God wants to heal nations and bring justice to the poor and oppressed.

## NOTES

1. Richard Lovelace, *Dynamics of Spiritual Life* (Downers Grove, Ill.: InterVarsity, 1979), 42, emphasis added.

2. Ibid., 368.

3. Ibid., 360–361.

4. Ibid., 361.

5. Ibid., 370.

6. www.brycchancarey.com/abolition/wesley.htm.

7. http://gbgm-umc.org/umw/wesley.

8. Lovelace, *Dynamics of Spiritual Life*, 370.

9. Quoted Timothy Smith, *Revivalism and Social Reform* (New York: Abingdon, 1957), 161.

10. Ibid.

11. Quoted in Ronald J. Sider and Diane Knippers, eds., *Toward an Evangelical Public Policy* (Grand Rapids, Mich.: Baker, 2005), 205.

12. Quoted in Smith, *Revivalism*, 205.

13. Seth Rees, *The Ideal Pentecostal Church* (Cincinnati: Knapp, 1897), 41.

14. Dr. Mitchell said this in a conversation with Tony Casey, assistant district superintendent of the South Carolina district of The Wesleyan Church, who told it to me.

15. Ellsworth Kalas, *The Asbury Herald,* 116/3 (Summer, 2006), 20.

16. Ronald J. Sider, *Rich Christians in an Age of Hunger* (Downers Grove, Ill.: InterVarsity, 1977), 203–204.

# HOLINESS AT THE GRASSROOTS LEVEL

*Tom Kinnan*

*Sanctify them by the truth; your word is truth. As you sent me into the world, I have sent them into the world. For them I sanctify myself, that they too may be truly sanctified.*

—John 17:17–19

*To the convinced, the life of holiness afforded the essence of freedom.*

—Charles Edwin Jones

I don't speak coffee. While my wife, Queenie, loves her trips to Starbucks, luxuriating in those small oases in the day and basking in sips of pure delight, I loathe that black, bitter drink. Queenie casually says, "One low-fat latte, one pump mocha, two Splenda." When I order for her, she has to repeat that to me every time because I don't retain such language. That vernacular is unnecessary in my world. And, as you know, when you don't speak the language—as I don't speak coffee—it can be difficult to communicate.

Therein lies one of the biggest challenges of communicating holiness to the people who sit in our churches. We don't always speak the same language, and many people view "holy talk" as being unnecessary in their worlds. Interestingly, many pastors have worked hard to learn the language of society but, in so doing, have forgotten how to translate biblical concepts to the nonbiblical public. Biblical language can seem foreign when we seldom use it. Scripturally, we know we are not citizens of this earth; we are immigrants, travelers passing through. Unfortunately, we have learned the language of culture better than we know what should be our native tongue. Obviously, that affects our ability to communicate holiness. It is imperative that we learn to understand God's Word and know how to translate it into language others can comprehend.

Remember the Where's Waldo? books and pictures? You look and look, but ol' Waldo is not easy to pick out. It's not unlike a dilemma we have in the church: It's becoming increasingly difficult to pick out men and women of God. What we do and who we are is more closely related to hedonism than to holiness. Not only our language, but also our actions, reflect the values of society more than the character of God.

Some individuals get upset with the church and the standards set there. It's not uncommon for churches to be accused of being too rigid or confining or judgmental. The "judgmental" accusation, which becomes equal to its own pronouncement, usually surfaces because the church has taken a biblical stand on an issue and, as such, it is not always sympathetic to an atmosphere of relative values. Many perceive biblical values to be judgmental and out of place in a tolerance-driven world.

People often misunderstand holiness, both inside and outside the church. Those outside easily can misconstrue it as a value of a religious subculture, not something for everyone. Similarly, some within the church think holiness is an elevated religious state reserved for the spiritually elite. If you are "holy," it is assumed you are a part of the special forces of Christianity. A related misconception is that to achieve such a lofty state requires entering into a level of perfection few ever attain. The reality is this: Holiness is the expected biblical norm for those who claim to walk with God. We as the church are called to communicate that by example and with conviction.

Preaching and promoting holy values, and living those values, are responsibilities of the church, because we are to be *about* holy living. Although I don't believe that generally our churches are shining "like stars in the universe" (Phil. 2:15) in our demonstration of holiness, we do desire, for the most part, to continue promoting scriptural holiness. That desire always must move from intentions of the heart and soul into practices that evidence the character and nature of God.

As we seek to evidence holiness in the church, aside from our preaching, four distinct emphases must rise to the top: forgiveness, relationships, service, and lifestyle.

## FORGIVENESS

Sometimes in a culture of relative values, pursuit of God can be construed as merely a search for a "higher power." Moreover, in the mind-set of a self-oriented society, pursuit of God does not necessarily mean pursuit of a transforming God who will alter an individual according to God's desires. Some "pursue God" to find ways to validate their own opinions and lifestyle, attempting to mold God to their own priorities and values.

However, when we seek the Lord, we are seeking holiness, even if we are not aware of it. Why? Because to walk with God is to walk with and in holiness. God is utterly holy. The essence of his being is untainted, pure, and without any sinful scars. We, on the other hand, enter life with a sinful nature and then proceed to mobilize that nature. As a result, we are covered with the scars of the sins that grow out of our "bent toward sinning."

I regularly engage with people who are licking their wounds and desperately seeking healing from pain. When people walk into the church, seldom are they focused on holiness. Instead, they usually are tuned in to their personal issues and stresses. It is not uncommon for people to be in search of relationships, counsel, financial assistance, comfort, or just about anything other than holiness. Most do not associate holiness with healing.

Yet—it bears repeating—holiness is the essence of the character of God, comprising the state in which he lives. Holiness repels sin. That is why holiness is central to healing. It not only removes the sin from us, but also restores our nature to one that leans more toward righteousness than toward ungodliness. That doesn't mean we are free of temptation or even free of any trace of sin. We often struggle with keeping Christ central in our lives, and may allow many kinds of ungodly attitudes and actions to interfere in our spiritual journey. But holiness, the presence of God, lives in us, fills us, possesses us; we have the "presence" of mind and heart to address God who enables us to address our behavior. God forgives, cleanses, and empowers.

We must seek to live this area of forgiveness demonstrably in the church. None of us lives for any amount of time without experiencing pain and rejection in relationships. But not only have we been hurt by others; we ourselves also have been the offenders, whether intentionally or unintentionally. We understand the need of forgiveness.

In communicating holiness, one of the frontline evidences is that we are not only forgiven, we are forgiving. Forgiveness is highly valued in the living out of holiness. Forgiveness erases sin. Forgiveness restores hope. I never cease to be amazed at the number of people who espouse holiness but harbor unforgiveness in their lives. When unforgiveness takes up residence, it does not allow us to extend grace to others. Self becomes more valued than others, contrary to biblical teaching, and worlds apart from the reality of holiness.

What is forgiveness? Forgiveness is the wronged individual's assumption of the consequences of the offense. What is done cannot be changed. The past cannot be undone. That means if you've wronged me and I forgive you, I accept whatever pain came my way and I, by choice, erase the wrong from your record. That's how Christ forgave me. He assumed the consequences for my sin and erased my guilt. In other words, by forgiving me, Jesus said he values me more than he values my sin. He let my sin go and holds on to me. When we fail to forgive, essentially we are communicating that we value a person's sin more than we value the person, since we choose to keep the sin and sever the relationship. Holiness holds on to what is right, not what is wrong.

Some say that to forgive means the offending party gets off with no consequences, and the response is, "It's not fair!" Of course it isn't. Nor do we want it to be fair. In a fair world, there are no such gifts as mercy and grace. We deserve neither. The last thing we want in life is fair. If life is fair, we are without hope.

Because of God's unfairness, because of his gifts of mercy and grace, I'm in the ministry. A holy God forgave me, an unholy man. And then he took up residence in me and made me holy by his presence and the power of his Spirit.

People need hope, and that hope is found in Christ and his holiness. Churches and people that do not practice forgiveness cannot claim to be holy. Unforgiveness is anathema to holiness. Forgiveness allows our relationship with God and with others to flourish.

## RELATIONSHIPS

When churches practice forgiveness, they are demonstrating another value central to holiness: healthy relationships. Holiness exists in the context of relationships. It is central to the character and nature of the Trinity, and, when we are surrendered to Christ, it is central to who we are. We cannot separate holiness from the presence of God. Wherever he dwells, holiness dwells. Thus, if I want to be holy, I must allow the Holy Spirit to indwell all of me so that I become holy by virtue of his presence.

But God is not simply residing in me; he is relating to me. His holiness permeates all my interactions with others, and should be spilling out into all my relationships. Holiness does not live on a remote island of religiosity. No, we communicate and live Christ in the context of relationships. God became a man and lived among us. Jesus was holiness in flesh and blood and modeling before us how the character of God is lived out in the nature of humanity.

We can see clearly that God values relationships, by the manner in which the Incarnate Christ entered the world. He came as the Son of God and made himself the Son of Man by entering through Mary's womb. He could have walked onto the scene as a sort of Melchizedek, or human theophany. He simply could have shown up one day as a fully grown man. Instead, Christ entered the world through existing relationships.

In my early years, it is safe to say, I was a very active child; my presence often created some level of upheaval in our home. In fact, often when I would walk into the house, my mom would look at me and say, "Calm down!" Now, that was before I ever spoke or did anything that would cause a disturbance.

On one occasion, our family was leaving to visit my grandparents. As we drove away from the house, Dad pulled out some letters that needed mailing, planning to deposit them in the mailbox at the end of the street. Naturally, I jumped into the picture, offering my assistance and begging to be allowed to be the one to deliver the mail into the postal receptor. When we arrived at the corner where the mailbox stood, my dad turned to me and began a fatherly lecture designed to help me focus on my appointed task—and, frankly, to preserve my life. You see, the mailbox was located across the street, which obviously necessitated a walk across pavement designed more for oncoming traffic than for hyperactive little boys. Dad instructed me to be sure to walk in front of his car and to look both ways before crossing. I responded with a "No kidding!" kind of look and snatched the mail from my father's hand.

In an instant I was out the car door. However, instead of going to the front of the car, I ran to the rear. In addition, I was more concerned with getting to the mailbox than with checking to see whether traffic would impede my progress. Thus, as I ran into the street I was met by a moving car that knocked me through the air, rendering me unconscious and lying on the curb.

When the car hit me, my dad turned to my mom and said, "What was the last thing I said to him?!"

She responded, "You told him to look both ways."

My dad then said, "I say leave him there and let him think about what he's done."

My mom chimed in, "Absolutely! When we come back maybe he'll be more open to listening and obeying."

You know my parents didn't do that. No, as soon as that car hit me, my parents were bolting out of the car and running to my side. They loved me and stood with me even when I had disobeyed. Love, and all that is right and holy, does not leave humanity lying in a pool of its own folly without offering help and hope. Why? Because relationships matter.

Some think God operates like the false response I gave of my parents. They think that, when they sin, God calls the angels in from the four corners of heaven and says, "What's the last thing I said to him?! I say let him wallow in his sin and we'll check on him later."

But that is not at all what happens. No! God rushes to our side to offer forgiveness and to pick us up. That is inherent in holiness. It lives and demonstrates what it seeks to establish: healthy relationships redeemed by the holy grace of God. Healthy relationships don't end because we stumble. They last because each partner in the relationship sees what it can become beyond the immediate moment. That is holiness in action. Holiness redeems not only an event; it redeems a person and relationships.

When people walk into our churches, they need to know that, regardless of what they've done or who they are, they are welcome in the presence of God. We need to extend holiness; we need to extend Christ. One way we do that is by offering them healthy, holy, lasting relationships.

## SERVICE

It's not uncommon for us to pick up theological insights from Charlie Brown, who seemed always to be encountering some life situation that mirrors the challenges we, too, face. One day, Charlie Brown just could not get his act together. He could not handle life, with its seeming lack of purpose or meaning, anymore. So he went to see Lucy for psychiatric help. Anyone who has ever read the *Peanuts* comic strip knows you have to be pretty desperate to seek out the counsel of Lucy. Nonetheless, Charlie Brown went to Lucy's psychiatric booth, where she dispensed her advice for the fee of five cents.

Charlie said, "Lucy, you are going to have to help me out. I don't know anything about my life. I don't have any meaning and purpose in it, and you are just going to have to help me put my act together."

Lucy looked at him in her know-it-all, sarcastic way and said, "Charlie Brown, life is like a deck chair on a ship. Some people take their deck chairs to the back of the ship, and they unfold them, and they sit there looking at where they have been. Other people take their deck chairs to the front of the ship to look and see where they are going." Then she said, "Charlie Brown, life is simple. Where is your deck chair?"

She looked at him in anticipation, and frustration was evident on his face. He scratched his head and said, "Lucy, I don't know, because I have never been able to get my deck chair unfolded."

That is the case for many Christians as it relates to the unfolding of practical holiness in their lives. There is no service. They got on the gospel ship, but they can't get their chairs unfolded. They can't seem to settle into the service of the King.

The ministry of the Incarnate God was holy service. He gave of himself wholly to humanity and desired that we would be set apart to serve. Christ prayed in the garden for the Father to "sanctify them" (John 17:17). He prayed that we would be distinguished, set apart, and recognizable because of our walk with God.

Then Jesus prayed, "I sanctify myself" (John 17:19). What did Christ mean when he said that? He couldn't have been talking about his own holiness. That's impossible. He was perfect from the beginning, without blemish. So what was he saying? He was talking about sanctification in its primary sense of being set apart, consecrated, dedicated. It's not about being made more moral or more ethical; it's about being completely surrendered and activated in service. It means a total offering of self to God for his glory and for his purpose.

The word *myself* has great significance. It means my total self: all that I am, all my privileges, relationships, abilities, possessions. "My whole being I offer to you, Father, for their sakes." Jesus was giving his all.

Holiness must be lived out in service to others. Sometimes those who have been enslaved by legalistic approaches to holiness have become frozen in their pews, afraid to move lest they sin or do something unholy. It's as though holiness is fragile and only operable when enclosed in a protective case and placed on a shelf. But that isn't holiness; that's laziness and fear. Holy living means humble serving. It means caring for the poor, lifting up the brokenhearted, looking out for splintered families, reaching out to the disenfranchised. Too often, we look at those around us who are hurting and say, "I'll pray for you." That's good, but God also expects us to extend a hand, a meal, a shoulder to lean on, a listening ear, a friendship, a coat—whatever we can offer to address the need in their lives.

Historically, compassionate ministries have been at the heart of the Holiness Movement. With a heart for the plight of the poor and disadvantaged, its participants launched missions and churches in the inner cities, hoping to change lives. They met with some success, but, since they were reaching the poor, fiscal solvency was always a challenge. In time, in spite of the differences being made, these churches, too, became more concerned about the condition of their children and the preservation of their churches. They came to believe they needed to be where the influences on their people were better and there were more financially equipped people to contribute to the cause.

"Self-support seemed inevitably to signal abandonment of mission work and desertion of downtown locations for residential neighborhoods."[1] Although urban flight was occurring, many who left continued to partner with independent missions that remained in the inner city and serve through them. Ironically, ministry to the poor was the badge of authenticity for most holiness upstarts. It is sad and convicting to me personally, when I read Charles Jones' statement, "Within twenty years of assuming denominational form, holiness churches officially abandoned welfare work."[2] While that may be a bit overstated, the reality is that churches continue to flee the inner city and leave the work to a handful of independent missions.

If we are serious about holiness, we must be serious about serving those around us and reaching out in a visible, tangible manner that gives glory to God.

## LIFESTYLE

It almost goes without saying that legalism has haunted the halls of holiness in our churches. In an effort to distinguish clearly those who are holy, external standards are sometimes taught as the evidence of being Spirit-filled. While, in most cases, I do not believe this was done to control others or somehow to blind the church to the reality of what God does, legalism has crippled countless individuals across the years.

A friend of mine who came out of a legalistic background told me of an experience he'd had. Life for many in the Holiness Movement is spent gazing into the ditches of the "cannots" instead of walking in the freedom of the "can do's." Sure enough, my friend had been taught all he shouldn't do if he wanted to be holy. Among other things, he couldn't wear rings, had to wear long sleeves, couldn't eat out on Sunday, couldn't read the Sunday paper, and, of course, couldn't watch TV on the Lord's Day.

One Sunday, as a true, red-blooded, gridiron fan, he discreetly turned on the TV to watch his team, the Pittsburgh Steelers. As it happened, when he turned the game on, the Steelers were winning. But in the short time he watched the game, the Steelers fell behind by three touchdowns. My friend quickly turned off the TV and went to prayer. He honestly believed that by watching the Steelers he was causing them to lose, because it was wrong of him to watch TV on Sunday. So he went and prayed the Lord would please help them regain the lead and win.

Now, we don't want to throw out the frames with the broken lens. My friend did understand that behavior outside God's will has consequences. Beyond that, he understood that such behavior can affect those around him adversely. However, he was misguided by focusing a positive understanding on nonessentials. God would not cause a football team to lose because one of its fans had violated a legalistic taboo.

Let me explain it in the context of self-control. When we were living in Central, South Carolina, I did a lot of traveling to churches all over the south. Often, I came home along I-85 late at night. Inevitably, it seemed, the highway was in the midst of construction, which meant that cement barriers formed walls along the road. Regularly, torrential rain would make it all the more difficult to see. Then, of course, with rain falling, I would be caught between a semi-trailer on one side of me and the cement wall on the other. My question was this: Where should I look, at the truck or the wall? Well, as you know, the answer is neither. I had to look straight ahead. If I had watched the wall or the truck, I would have hit one of them. Self-control is the ability to watch where you should be going, not where you shouldn't be going.

That is the practical unfolding of lifestyle holiness. It is watching where we should be going. It is focusing on the "can do's." It is picking up the cross that compels rather than picking up a cross that discourages. A holy lifestyle will reflect some activities in which we don't participate. But the issue is not always that we are against the activity, as much as we are for something that has higher value. In college one of my professors was asked if drinking is a sin. I'll never forget his answer. He said, "Drinking is so far down on my list of priorities that it doesn't come into question." He was looking forward, and his actions were played out in the context of what he stood for, not what he stood against.

Lifestyle holiness stands for Christ. Now, please don't misunderstand and think it is not our responsibility to address what is wrong. We must do that. But to fail to have a balance between that and focusing on where we must be going leads to legalism and to a church that fails to act.

Holiness always will be here. Why? Because God will not go away; His character will not fade. And he wants the character of holiness to live in us. That character is clearly visible in how we practice forgiveness, nurture healthy relationships, engage in humble service, and live lifestyles that give evidence that Christ lives in us and we are moving forward in a holy journey with him. We are not beyond holiness, because we are not beyond God. Let's live in the security and freedom of the essence of God: holiness.

## ACTION/REFLECTION SUGGESTIONS

**1.** Examine your church and ministry. What would make it distinguishable as a church that says holiness is a priority?

**2.** If your church closed or moved from your community, would the community notice or care? What difference is the holiness of God making in your community through your church?

**3.** What has this chapter crystallized for you in terms of your understanding of holiness? Who else in your church needs to read and ponder it?

## NOTES

1. Charles Edwin Jones, *Perfectionist Persuasion* (Scarecrow Press, 1974), 127.
2. Ibid., 137.

# EPILOGUE

You have just have finished this survey of a Wesleyan understanding of holiness. You've been reinforced in your understanding that holiness is a thoroughly biblical concept, one of the Bible's central teachings. You've been reminded of the importance of holiness, rightly understood, and that holiness is not just for a few super-saints, but is God's intention for every one of God's children.

You have seen again (or perhaps for the first time) how John and Charles Wesley came to rediscover holiness, and their theological and practical genius in making holiness a central theme of the Methodist movement as it swept the British Isles and North America in the eighteenth and early nineteenth centuries. You were reminded of the ups and downs of holiness thinking in American Methodism and its offshoots. You rejoiced at the rediscovery of holiness outside traditional Wesleyan circles, and at the many ways God works to revitalize holiness understanding, experience, and teaching within them. (That's us, and we need revitalizing, too!)

We've considered together holiness from a number of vantage points, and discovered again that holiness is personal, but also corporate; individually purifying, but also the only motivation for social justice that is both genuine and on-going. If you have regular opportunities to preach, you've been (I hope) energized to re-examine and renew your desire and commitment to preach biblical holiness because you and the people you shepherd need it.

You've been reminded that holiness is a diamond—every genuine facet is awesome and breathtakingly beautiful. You've been reaffirmed in your conviction that holiness is not a secret gnostic doctrine, but the expression of the intimate, even passionate, relationship God desires with every daughter and son brought into God's family through the Incarnation, the redeeming death, and the hope-engendering Resurrection of Jesus Christ, our Elder Brother and Hero.

Now, what are you and I going to do about it? How will we be different tomorrow because of what we've read and pondered here? How will this book affect our reading, study, and preaching of the Bible? How will we think differently? How will we look at people differently, and how will we treat them differently? How will we do differently what we've been doing outside the pulpit, and what will we begin to do that we haven't been doing?

God's perfect Shalom upon and through you—upon and through each and all of us—as we respond to God's holiness, God's everlastingly faithful lovingkindness toward us in Christ, through the Holy Spirit.

If not godly, biblical, Christian holiness, then what? If not now, then when?

JOSEPH COLESON

# FOR FURTHER READING

**Blevins, Dean G.** "'Holy Church, Holy People': A Wesleyan Exploration in Congregational Holiness and Personal Testament," *Wesleyan Theological Journal* 39, no. 2 (2004): 54–73.

In this interesting and important article, Blevins examines ecclesial holiness in terms of "embodiment," a reference to both personal and social bodies.

**Brauer, Jerald.** *Protestantism in America.* Philadelphia: Westminster, 1972.

This text, used in many colleges and seminaries, provides a broader overview of the various traditions and denominational groups that have shaped American Christianity. The text is available online.

**Bridges, Jerry.** *The Pursuit of Holiness.* Colorado Springs: Navpress, 2006.

In the last twenty-five years, few books have contributed more to the growing interest in holiness than this book by Jerry Bridges. While he is not a proponent of "the shorter way" into holiness, no person serious about holiness can ignore this "longer way" approach to holiness that has been so recently popular.

**Cattell, Everett L.** *The Spirit of Holiness.* Kansas City: Beacon Hill Press, 1963.

This little book offers a straightforward approach to the issue of holiness.

**Coleson, Joseph,** ed. *The Church Jesus Builds: A Dialogue on the Church in the 21st Century.* Indianapolis: Wesleyan, 2007.

Two chapters in particular relate to social/corporate/community holiness, one by Keith Drury on corporate spirituality (encapsulating his recently published book, listed below) and the other by Ken Schenck on the book of Acts as a template for the Spirit-led church.

**Dayton, Donald.** *Discovering an Evangelical Heritage.* Peabody, Mass.: Hendrickson, 1988.

Dayton's book is a classic that gives a compelling historical basis for the integration of faith and engagement in the culture. This updated edition is essential reading for all in the Wesleyan tradition, as much of the history of Wesleyan social action, "holiness and justice," is here.

__________. *Theological Roots of Pentecostalism.* Peabody, Mass.: Hendrickson, 1991.

Although most Wesleyans would consider themselves in opposition to much of the teaching of modern-day Pentecostalism, Dayton shows how the emphasis upon the baptism of the Holy Spirit in nineteenth-century holiness preaching shifted, over several decades, into the major themes that underlie the modern Pentecostal and Charismatic movements.

**Dieter, Melvin E., Anthony A. Hoekema, Stanley M. Horton, J. Robertson McQuilkin, and John F. Walvoord.** *Five Views on Sanctification.* Grand Rapids, Mich.: Zondervan, 1987.

A balanced, give-and-take dialogue between the main Protestant positions on sanctification. Melvin Dieter has written a concise, reasoned description of the Wesleyan perspective, and deals with the main scriptural passages for its support.

**Drury, Keith.** Full of optimism for God's changing grace, this book promotes "the shorter way" of entire sanctification in an era when few believe such a powerful work of grace is possible to receive in a short time. *Holiness for Ordinary People*. Indianapolis: Wesleyan, 2004.

__________. *Disciplines of Holy Living*. Indianapolis: Wesleyan, 1989.

Drury's first book on spiritual discipline lays a groundwork for understanding and practicing eight personal disciplines. This is a practical tool to help anyone bring Christ into daily life.

__________. *There Is No I in Church.* Indianapolis: Wesleyan, 2006.

Offering a corrective desperately needed in today's church, this is a must-read for Christians in an age increasingly preoccupied with privatized faith.

__________. *With Unveiled Faces*. Indianapolis: Wesleyan, 2005.

This book introduces thirteen spiritual disciplines. Drury helps the seeker explore and develop habits that will assist the pursuit of wholeness in Christ.

**Foster, Richard J.** *Celebration of Discipline: The Path to Spiritual Growth.* New York: HarperCollins, 1978.

Foster's classic work is a must for every believer. He covers twelve spiritual disciplines and provides guidance to get started.

**Greenway, Jeffrey E.**, and Joel B. Green, eds. *Grace and Holiness in a Changing World: A Wesleyan Proposal for Postmodern Ministry.* Nashville: Abingdon, 2007.

The Wesleyan message speaks powerfully to a world in flux. See especially Howard Snyder's chapter, "Holiness of Heart and Life in a Postmodern World."

**Gushee, David, with Glen H. Stassen.** *Kingdom Ethics: Following Jesus in Contemporary Context.* Downers Grove, IL: InterVarsity, 2003.

This book focuses on the Sermon on the Mount to define the kingdom of God and to develop a basis for moral decisions. This approach then is applied to contemporary issues.

**Haines, Lee, and Paul Thomas.** *An Outline History of The Wesleyan Church.* Indianapolis: Wesleyan, 2005.

Including the Wesleyan Revival in England to the current day, this is a compilation of materials written by the historians of the two denominations that merged in 1968 to form The Wesleyan Church.

**Hurley, Michael,** ed. *John Wesley's Letter to a Roman Catholic.* Nashville: Abingdon, 1968.

Hurley's edition of Wesley's "Letter to a Roman Catholic" sets the letter in its historical and theological context.

**Jones, Charles Edwin.** *Perfectionist Persuasion.* Lanham: Scarecrow, 1974.

This book provides a good historical overview of the early Holiness Movement in America.

**Küng, Hans.** *On Being a Christian.* New York: Doubleday, 1977.

An apologetic treatise by a prominent Roman Catholic theologian, this book was written to suggest why the person of Jesus Christ still is worthy to be followed, even in a global and secularly humanistic world.

**Law, William.** *A Serious Call to a Devout and Holy Life.* Mahwah: Paulist Press, 1978.

William Law had a significant influence on John Wesley's thinking regarding the possibility of living life with a purity of intentions. This book is as readable today as it was centuries ago and is available free online at http://www.nnu.edu/wesley/index.htm.

**Lewis, Robert.** *The Church of Irresistible Influence.* Grand Rapids: Zondervan, 2003.

This is the story of one church's adventure in demonstrating the love of Christ in and to their community. It is an excellent model for any church to follow to mobilize holy compassion in its community.

**Lodahl, Michael.** *The Story of God: Wesleyan Theology and Biblical Narrative*. Kansas City: Beacon Hill Press, 1994.

This book covers theological issues in all of Scripture, and part of it addresses issues of holiness in the New Testament.

**Lyon, Jo Anne.** *The Ultimate Blessing*. Indianapolis: Wesleyan, 2003.

Jo Anne's gift for storytelling comes through as she recounts her journey of putting her faith into action. This book is both practical and inspirational and helps the reader get a picture of practical holiness.

**Marshall, I. Howard.** *New Testament Theology: Many Witnesses, One Gospel*. Downers Grove, IL: InterVarsity, 2004.

Marshall is a respected New Testament scholar who is a British Methodist. This book represents the fruit of many years teaching and writing, and though quite long and detailed, it is clearly written and will well repay study.

**Moberg, David O.** *The Great Reversal: Evangelism versus Social Concern*. Philadelphia: Lippincott, 1972.

This book provides a historical overview of how the early holiness churches engaged in social concerns, and then turned their backs and walked away. It is convicting and enlightening, a must-read.

**Nouwen, Henri J. M.**, Donald P. McNeill, and Douglas A. Morrison. *Compassion: A Reflection on Christian Life*. New York: Image, 1983.

The book focuses on the self-emptying (*kenotic*) love necessary to serve Christ. We are set apart and empowered to serve, by dying to self and living by the power of the Spirit. An excellent read, provocative and challenging.

**Oord, Thomas Jay, and Michael Lodahl.** *Relational Holiness: Responding to the Call of Love*. Kansas City: Beacon Hill Press, 2005.

Complete with study questions, this very accessible book examines love as the "core" of holiness. The chapter on corporate holiness stands out, as does the chapter on the relationships within the Trinity as a model for our relationships in the body of Christ.

**Ortberg, John.** *The Life You've Always Wanted: Spiritual Disciplines for Ordinary People*. Grand Rapids: Zondervan, 2004.

This is a book, but it also comes as a video curriculum of six sessions, and workbooks are available (and recommended). It is great for adult Sunday school classes or small groups.

**Oswalt, John N.** *Called to be Holy.* Nappanee, IN: Evangel, 1999.

This is a fairly easy-to-read but well-informed book, and Oswalt does not try to be comprehensive, but instead offers helpful explanations of selected key Scripture passages from both Old and New Testaments.

**Palmer, Phoebe.** *Entire Devotion to God.*

If John Wesley is the father of the Methodist/Holiness Movement, certainly Phoebe Palmer is our mother, at least in America. This book, first published in 1847, is an excellent example of the "optimism of grace" typical of Methodist/Holiness leaders from the mid-1800s. Unfortunately, it is out of print today. However, the entire book is available free online; search by author at http://www.nnu.edu/wesley/index.htm.

**Purkiser, W. T.** *Exploring Christian Holiness*, vol. 1: *The Biblical Foundations.* Kansas City: Beacon Hill Press, 1983.

This book offers a detailed discussion of many important biblical passages relating to holiness. Written from a Nazarene perspective, it is useful for those who want more exegetical detail.

**Runyon, Theodore.** *The New Creation: John Wesley's Theology Today.* Nashville: Abingdon, 1998.

This is a contemporary survey of John Wesley's theology that uses Christian perfection ("the new creation") as the central, principal theme of his work.

**Sider, Ronald J.**, and Diane Knippers, eds. *Toward an Evangelical Public Policy*. Grand Rapids: Baker, 2005.

This book provides an evangelical framework for public engagement. In addition, a short booklet, *For the Health of the Nation: An Evangelical Call to Civic Responsibility*, is included at the end of the book. It also can be downloaded from the NAE website, as well as ordered in hard copy from the Web site www.NAE.net.

**Smith, Timothy.** *Revivalism and Social Reform.* New York: Harper Torchbooks, 1957.

Smith, a scholar from The Church of the Nazarene, provides a sound case for merging holiness doctrine with activism, with a view to changing both individuals and social structures.

**Tyson, John R.** *Charles Wesley: A Reader*. Oxford: Oxford University Press, 1989.

Tyson gives us a fascinating look at the brilliant thinking of the *other* Wesley brother.

__________. *Charles Wesley on Sanctification: A Theological and Biographical Study*. Grand Rapids, MI: Zondervan, 1986 (reprinted by Schmul).

This is a detailed study of Charles Wesley's theology of holiness. Of particular interest, perhaps, is the way it compares and contrasts with that of John Wesley.

__________. *Invitation to Christian Spirituality: An Ecumenical Anthology*. Oxford University Press, 1999.

This book is a great introduction to the history of Christianity through the primary sources of Christian praxis and spirituality.

**Ware, Timothy.** *The Orthodox Church*. New York: Penguin, 1997.

__________. *The Orthodox Way*. New York: St. Vladimir's Seminary Press, 1995.

These two books by Timothy Ware, now Bishop Kallistos, are the best entry to date into the Orthodox tradition.

**Wesley, John.** *A Plain Account of Christian Perfection*. Kansas City: Barefoot Ministries, 2005.

With Wesley's engaging question-and-answer approach, this booklet is perhaps the best introduction ever of the foundational approach to the notion of "full salvation." It can be accessed (and copied) online by searching the author at http://www.nnu.edu/wesley/index.htm.

**Whitney, Donald.** *Spiritual Disciplines for the Christian Life*. Colorado Springs: Navpress, 1991.

This resource includes the more common disciplines but also includes evangelism.

**Willard, Dallas.** *Renovation of the Heart*. Colorado Springs: NavPress, 2002.

Willard has become perhaps the most important voice in evangelical America in terms of authentic discipleship. His grasp of the human heart, and how the Scriptures detail God's provision for it, is nothing short of amazing.

**Wright, N. Thomas.** *The Challenge of Jesus: Rediscovering Who Jesus Was and Is*. Downers Grove, Ill.: InterVarsity, 1999.

This and other books in the series of the same name are recommended for their readability. Wright, a gifted New Testament scholar who has taught at Oxford and is now an Anglican bishop, uses everyday illustrations and down-to-earth language to help readers grasp afresh the meaning of Scripture.

___________. *Paul for Everyone: 1 Corinthians.* Louisville: Westminster, 2004.

This book will help the reader understand better what Jesus' message meant to his Jewish audience, and may throw new light on the significance of some of his sayings or deeds.

**Wynkoop, Mildred Bangs.** *A Theology of Love: The Dynamic of Wesleyanism.* Kansas City: Beacon Hill Press, 1972.

Mildred Wynkoop gave the church a new paradigm in this classic of holiness literature, proposing a relational view of sanctification. Holiness scholarship has been in her debt ever since.

# ABOUT THE AUTHORS

**Clarence Bence** (most friends call him "Bud") is Vice President and Academic Dean for the College of Arts and Sciences at Indiana Wesleyan University. Bud spent his childhood in upstate New York, where his father was a pastor and district superintendent in The Wesleyan Church. After studies at Houghton College and Asbury Seminary, Bud became pastor of the Penfield, New York, Wesleyan Church, where he developed a large youth program and a congregation open to the "Jesus Movement" of the early 1970s. After five years in Penfield, he enrolled in the doctoral program at Emory University, and earned a Ph.D. in Wesley Studies.

For the past twenty-five years, Dr. Bence has devoted himself to teaching in Wesleyan colleges—first at United Wesleyan College, then at Indiana Wesleyan University (formerly Marion College). In addition to his ministry in the classroom, he has served as Academic Dean at both Houghton College and Indiana Wesleyan University. He has authored a commentary on the book of Romans in a multi-volume series produced by Wesleyan Publishing House, and was one of the editors of the *Reflecting God Study Bible*.

Bud is married to Carol, who is Director of Nursing Programs in Indiana Wesleyan University's College of Adult and Professional Studies. The Bences have three grown children.

**Robert Black** is a third-generation Wesleyan minister. Since 1986, he has been a member of the religion faculty at Southern Wesleyan University; for ten years he served as chair of the division. A graduate of Southern Wesleyan University, he also earned the M.Div. degree from Asbury Theological Seminary, and a Ph.D. in Church History from Union Theological Seminary, Richmond, Virginia.

Bob has been a contributor to the Wesleyan Bible Commentary Series (1 & 2 Timothy); to *Reformers and Revivalists*, the denominational history of The Wesleyan Church; and to several reference works in his field. *How Firm a Foundation*, his history of Southern Wesleyan, was published for the University's centennial celebration in 2006.

Bob and his wife, Judy, are the parents of Jon, Jenny, and Jared, and the grandparents of Olivia, the world's grandest grandchild.

**Joseph Coleson** is a native of western Michigan. His BA is from Indiana Wesleyan University, his MA and Ph.D. degrees from Brandeis University. Since 1995, he has been Professor of Old Testament at Nazarene Theological Seminary, and an adjunct professor at the University of Missouri, Kansas City; he is a Fellow of the Wesley Studies Centre, University of Manchester. Previously, he served on the faculties of Roberts Wesleyan College and Western Evangelical Seminary. Joseph was ordained in The Wesleyan Church in 1979; he has pastoral experience in two Conferences of the United Methodist Church.

Joseph is editor of this series, Wesleyan Theological Perspectives, and of Nazarene Theological Seminary's academic journal. He recently finished a commentary on Joshua for the *Cornerstone Biblical Commentary* (Tyndale), and is working on Genesis for a new commentary series from Beacon Hill. Joseph is a frequent contributor to adult Christian education curricula.

Joseph enjoys family life with his wife, Charlotte, a retired elementary-education reading specialist, and time with their two grown children and their spouses, and with two lively, lovely grandchildren. Reading mystery novels and gardening are two of his other interests.

**Keith Drury** teaches practical ministry courses at Indiana Wesleyan University, where he focuses his time raising up the next generation of ministers for the Church. He is the author of a variety of books, including *Holiness for Ordinary People*, which continues to enjoy brisk sales more than twenty-five years after it was written. His most recent book, on the Apostle's Creed, emphasizes the common ground all Christians share in our beliefs. During the school year, Keith writes a weekly "Tuesday Column" that has been posted on the Internet since 1995.

Keith lives in Marion, Indiana, with his wife, Sharon, who teaches in Indiana Wesleyan University's doctoral program in leadership. An avid backpacker, Keith has completed both the Appalachian Trail and the Pacific Crest Trail, and has logged more than 10,000 miles on trails in America and Europe. Sharon goes backpacking with him, but not for longer than one week at a time. Keith and Sharon are the parents of David Drury and John Drury; together with their spouses, both are involved significantly in ministry in and through The Wesleyan Church.

**Richard Eckley** is an ordained minister in The Wesleyan Church and Associate Professor of Theology at Houghton College, Houghton, New York. He also serves part-time as Assistant to the Pastor of The Wesleyan Church of Orchard Park, New York. Dr. Eckley holds the BS degree from United Wesleyan College, the M.Div. from Asbury Theological Seminary, and the Th.M. from Princeton Theological Seminary. His dissertation for the Ph.D. from Duquesne University was a study of pneumatology in current ecumenical theology.

Rich was a contributor to the first volume of this series, *Passion, Power, and Purpose: Essays on the Art of Contemporary Preaching*. In 2006, Wesleyan Publishing House published his commentary, *Revelation: A Commentary for Bible Students*.

This past year, Rich and his wife, Lynn, married off both their sons to two gifted and beautiful Houghton College graduates.

**David Holdren** is Executive Pastor of The Cypress Wesleyan Church of Columbus, Ohio. He is a graduate of Owosso College, of Asbury Theological Seminary, and of Ball State University.

Dave's primary vocational passion and experience is that of pastor. Along the way he has served as an interim district superintendent, as executive editor of curriculum for The Wesleyan Church, and as a General Superintendent for five years. He is pleased to have been the first person ever elected directly from a pastoral role to the general superintendency.

Dave and his wife, Marlene, have two grown daughters, Marsha and Amy, and four fantastic grandchildren. Dave's hobbies include motorcycling, both on-road and off-road; racquetball; and backpacking.

**Judy Huffman** is Pastor of Congregational Life at College Wesleyan Church, Marion, Indiana. She began this pastoral role two years ago, following God's call to parish ministry. Prior to this, she spent sixteen years on the faculty of Indiana Wesleyan University. She taught for twelve years and spent the last four years as Dean of the College of Arts and Sciences. Judy earned her master's degree in Counseling from Clemson University, and a doctorate in Counseling from the University of Georgia. Dr. Huffman is a licensed Marriage and Family Therapist, and is currently working toward ministerial ordination in The Wesleyan Church.

Six great-nephews and one great-niece, ages six months to ten years, bless Judy's life. She has a terrific extended family and they remain one of her greatest joys. As a single woman, she also is thankful for dear friends who bring her into their families as one of their own.

**Tom Kinnan** has been a pastor for thirty-one of his thirty-five years in ministry. He has been pastor of BreakPointe Community Church in Overland Park, Kansas, since its inception in 2002.

Tom completed a Bachelor of Arts degree at Marion College (now Indiana Wesleyan University) in 1974. He spent one quarter doing undergraduate work at Jerusalem University College, Jerusalem, Israel (1972). Tom received the Master of Ministry degree from Anderson (Indiana) School of Theology (1976), and did further graduate studies at Indiana Wesleyan University (1989, 1993). After completing the M.Div. equivalency (non-degree) from Nazarene Theological Seminary in 2003, Tom enrolled in the Doctor of Ministry program at Nazarene Theological Seminary, Kansas City, earning his D.Min. degree in 2007.

Tom has been married to Kathy ("Queenie") for thirty-five years. They have two married children, both in ministry, and three grandchildren. Tom loves adventure, be it in sports, travel, or any undertaking that adds new understanding to life. Most of all, his family owns his heart and fills his life with contentment and joy.

**Jo Anne Lyon** was ordained in the Tri-State District of The Wesleyan Church in 1996. She earned her Bachelor's degree at the University of Cincinnati and her Master's at the University of Missouri, Kansas City. She did further work in theology at Saint Louis University and holds several honorary degrees, as well. Dr. Lyon is best known as the founder of World Hope, International, a relief and aid agency. From establishing medical clinics to distributing aid funds, she has led World Hope to become a diversified organization meeting the needs of others and empowering them to achieve a better life. Dr. Lyon has been recognized as an "agent of peace and reconciliation," and a change agent in the United States and many other countries.

Dr. Lyon has been involved in pastoral ministry in the local church setting, both inner-city and suburban. She preaches on college campuses, at retreats, in revival services, and in multi-denominational conventions. She preaches internationally, as well, in Africa, Asia, Europe, Australia, and Latin America.

Jo Anne enjoys playing softball with her five grandchildren, and discovering out-of-the-way "greasy spoon" restaurants with her husband, Wayne.

**Terence Paige** holds the BA degree from Seattle Pacific University; the MCS and the M.Div. degrees from Regent College, Vancouver, BC, Canada; and the Ph.D. from the University of Sheffield, Sheffield, England. He has taught in Belfast, Northern Ireland, and for the past fourteen years at Houghton College, Houghton, New York.

Dr. Paige's academic publications have appeared in the *Encyclopedia of the Historical Jesus* (Taylor & Francis), the *Dictionary of Paul and His Letters* (IVP), the *Dictionary of the Later New Testament* (IVP), and several scholarly journals, including the *Harvard Theological Review*. In addition, he has written studies for adult Sunday school publications of The Wesleyan Church, the Church of the Nazarene, and the United Methodist Church. He is involved in training adults for ministry in the FLAME program of The Wesleyan Church and in Houghton College's Equipping for Ministry program. He is currently working on a commentary on 1 & 2 Thessalonians for Beacon Hill Press.

Terence is married to Tracy, a Physical Therapist; they have three children. They enjoy travel to historic sites, gardening, museums, and walking their two dogs.

**John R. Tyson** is a native of Pittsburgh, Pennsylvania, and an avid fan of the Steelers and Pirates. He is Professor of Theology at Houghton College, Houghton, New York. John is an ordained minister in the United Methodist Church. He served several pastorates prior to earning his Ph.D. in Theological and Religious Studies at Drew University. He also is an alumnus of Grove City College, and of Asbury Theological Seminary.

An expert in Wesleyan Studies, Dr. Tyson has produced several books, including *Charles Wesley on Sanctification: A Biographical and Theological Study* (Zondervan, 1986); *Charles Wesley: A Reader* (Oxford University Press, 1989); and *Assist Me to Proclaim: Charles Wesley's Life and Hymns*, (Wm. B. Eerdmans Publishing Co., 2007). He has authored more than three dozen scholarly articles, which have appeared in various academic journals and church publications.

**J. Michael Walters** is Professor of Christian Ministries, Chair of the Department of Religion and Philosophy, and Director of Graduate Theological Studies, at Houghton College, Houghton, New York. He is also Director of Ministerial Education at Houghton, where he teaches preaching and advises ministerial students. Mike earned a B.A. degree from Circleville Bible College, a B.A. from Houghton College, an M.A.R. from Asbury Theological Seminary, an M.A. from St. Mary's University, and a D.Min. from Trinity Evangelical Divinity School.

Mike is an ordained minister in The Wesleyan Church and spent eighteen years in pastoral ministry, including thirteen years as senior pastor to the Houghton College campus and the community of Houghton, before joining the faculty of Houghton College.